Moving On After Childhood Sexual Abuse

This self-help guide allows those who have experienced childhood sexual abuse to consider the impact that it has had on their adult lives from a new perspective, helping them to understand the effects, and prepare for therapy.

Based on known reactions to physical and emotional trauma, this book explains how a broad range of difficulties in adulthood can result from sexual abuse in childhood. The reader is invited to think about how psychological therapy can be particularly helpful in reducing these difficulties and promoting change. Ground rules for therapy are provided, as well as guidance on how to get the most from the therapy process.

Moving On After Childhood Sexual Abuse provides a clear explanation of the developmental effects of childhood sexual abuse as well as the role of psychological therapy. This book will therefore assist the reader in making informed decisions about seeking treatment and setting personal goals for therapy, as well as appreciating the demands involved in the process of change.

Dr Jonathan Willows is a Chartered Clinical Psychologist, working in the NHS.

Moving On After Childhood Sexual Abuse

Understanding the Effects and
Preparing for Therapy

Jonathan Willows

Routledge
Taylor & Francis Group

LONDON AND NEW YORK

First published 2009 by Routledge
27 Church Road, Hove, East Sussex BN3 2FA

Simultaneously published in the USA and Canada
by Routledge
270 Madison Avenue, New York, NY, 10016

Routledge is an imprint of the Taylor & Francis Group, an Informa business

© 2009 Jonathan Willows

Typeset in Times by Garfield Morgan, Swansea, West Glamorgan
Printed and bound in Great Britain by TJ International Ltd, Padstow, Cornwall
Paperback cover design by Andy Ward

This publication has been produced with paper manufactured to strict environmental standards and with pulp derived from sustainable forests.

British Library Cataloguing in Publication Data
Willows, Jonathan, 1965-
  Moving on after childhood sexual abuse : understanding the effects and preparing for therapy / Jonathan Willows.
       p. cm.
  Includes bibliographical references and index.
  ISBN 978-0-415-42482-0 (hardback) – ISBN 978-0-415-42483-7 (pbk.) 1. Adult child sexual abuse victims–Rehabilitation. 2. Adult child sexual abuse victims–Mental health. I. Title.
  RC569.5.A28W55 2008
  616.85'83690651–dc22

                                                    2008008360

ISBN: 978-0-415-42482-0 (hbk)
ISBN: 978-0-415-42483-7 (pbk)

Contents

Acknowledgements

I would like to thank the many people who have helped me to produce this book. This includes tutors, supervisors, colleagues and the people with whom I have worked in clinical practice.

I am also indebted to those whose work provides the basis of our knowledge and practice in relation to mental health, psychological therapy and our current understanding of the devastating effects of childhood sexual abuse. I have cited and credited their work throughout the book and encourage interested readers to seek out the source material for themselves.

Dr Jonathan Willows
Clinical Psychologist

Part I

Childhood sexual abuse: an introduction and overview

1 Introduction: about this book and how to use it

This book is intended for anyone who has suffered sexual abuse as a child or adolescent. If this is something you have experienced, then this book will help you to consider some of the possible links between events in your past and some of the difficulties you may have as an adult. Furthermore, if you are thinking about going into therapy, this book is specifically intended to help you make informed decisions about what is most likely to help you. Thinking about this in advance, and considering the options, will help you get the most from therapy if you decide to proceed.

In order to decide what is right for you, it is important to have good information. This book provides it in a number of ways. Firstly, sexual abuse will be clearly defined. Then you will be provided with an overview of child development. This will help you to go on to think about what can happen when child development is disrupted by events such as sexual abuse. Then we will consider how adults continue to develop throughout their lives. At regular points you will be asked to stop and think about what you have read and about how it applies to you as a unique individual.

If you are considering going into therapy, several different types of psychological therapy will be described to help you to decide what is right for you. Making sure you have a good understanding of therapy and what is expected of you as a client is a good way to 'prepare' for therapy. Taking the time to complete the exercises at the end of the sections will also help you to get started on the road to change.

The book is presented in Parts I–IV, each of which is broken down into a number of chapters.

Part I provides a definition of sexual abuse and summarises its impact upon both child and adult development. This provides the starting point for considering how certain problems related to childhood sexual abuse can have a knock-on effect in other areas in one's life. This relationship will be explored in more detail later in the book, and we will see how psychological therapy can help to make positive changes.

Part II is about child development. It goes into more detail by exploring the many ways in which abusive experiences in childhood can affect growth and development. It describes some of the signs and symptoms that tell us, early on, that something is wrong. We will also continue to explore the idea that difficulties in childhood can build up over time and lead to additional difficulties in adulthood.

Part III is about adult development. It provides more information about the possible links between problems in childhood and related difficulties in adulthood. By drawing out the links between childhood trauma and the symptoms that occur in adults, some of these problems can be seen as *normal reactions to abnormal circumstances*. When people suffer extreme stress and are hurt, scared and confused, it can affect them in profound ways. The traumatic aspects of childhood sexual abuse are described here and the ongoing after-effects are explained. Having an explanation for how one feels can be a very important support in its own right. However, it is important to remember that the relationship between childhood sexual abuse and difficulties in adult life is not always straightforward. As discussed in more depth, not everyone who has been abused develops the same issues. Equally, not everyone who experiences the difficulties described has been abused. Some people remember very clearly what happened to them, others have an idea that 'something happened' – this does not *prove* that it did. In Part III, we will proceed with caution so that any conclusions you reach are based on sound judgement and real memories.

Part IV is all about therapy. It describes some of the more popular and readily available types of psychological therapy. There are some very important general issues to consider before going into therapy of any kind, and they are also described in detail here. This information will help you to make informed decisions about the type of therapy and the type of therapist most likely to help you. It should also help you to consider when the time is right to go ahead with therapy.

A number of people drop out of therapy early on. This can be for any number of reasons, including a lack of information about the different types of psychological therapy and how they work. Sometimes unrealistic expectations can get in the way, and sometimes it is just 'bad timing'. Others drop out because they are not prepared for the demands of therapy and for the amount of emotional work involved. Dropping out can be a disheartening experience and can undermine your hope for the future. Having sound information about what therapy involves can help you to avoid this. As an aid to this, some of the technical terms and jargon that are used in describing psychological therapy are also explained along the way. More importantly, Part IV also gives you some essential 'ground rules' for making sure that you get the most from therapy. These apply both to your therapist and to you as a client. They will help to ensure that you find your way to professionally accredited therapists who work in a way that is most likely to suit you. The ground rules are also there to help you to prepare for therapy by being mindful of the hard work and some of the potential pitfalls involved.

At frequent intervals throughout the book you will also find suggestions and prompts about how you can begin the process of thinking through what you want to get from therapy in more detail. You will also be encouraged to reflect on how you feel the information in each Part applies to you *as an individual*. By working through the book in this way you will be starting off the process of change and giving yourself a better chance of benefiting from therapy in the long run.

As you go through the book you may, of course, decide not to enter therapy at all or to put the idea to one side for the time being. It is better to use the information here to make an informed decision rather than just avoid 'change' because of fear or misinformation. Of course, it is also important to recognise that there are many other paths to achieving change and well-being besides psychological therapy.

Finally, the Further Information, Links and Contacts section at the back of the book provides signposts to various useful organisations and sources of information. This is followed by a list of references. The references are not 'essential' reading. They are simply there if you wish to find out more about something that has caught your attention along the way.

Throughout the book there are numerous case histories and examples. They are presented to help bring some of the ideas and theories to life. They also emphasise how broad and how varied some of the difficulties caused by childhood sexual abuse can be and how different stories can unfold. However, the examples will only reflect the experiences of some readers. Because everyone is an individual, it is also certainly not the case that 'one size fits all' when it comes to therapy or to getting over past events. The aim of this book is to help you to think carefully about what is right for *you* as an individual before going ahead.

A note of caution – how has childhood sexual abuse affected your life?

Throughout this book you will find descriptions of many different kinds of symptoms and psychological difficulties that can affect both children and adults. It is *very important* to recognise that each of them has many possible causes. Childhood sexual abuse is only one possible cause. Furthermore, in many cases, childhood sexual abuse is one difficulty amongst several others in a person's life. It is very important, therefore, to be as clear as you can about the impact that childhood sexual abuse has had upon you.

Generally speaking, there are three broad categories of people seeking therapy for the kinds of difficulties described in this book and who also believe that childhood sexual abuse has affected them:

- People who can clearly remember abuse happening to them and who feel sure that this has been a major factor in contributing to their difficulties as adults.
- People who can clearly remember abuse happening to them but who also recognise that this was one of several problems that have continued to affect them.
- People who do not remember being abused but who either believe it did happen to them *or* that it provides an 'explanation' for their current difficulties.

People in the first two groups will benefit from reading through this book and may well benefit from therapy aimed at alleviating some of the long-term effects of childhood sexual abuse. Of course, for those in the second group, this may be as part of a range of treatments for other difficulties.

People in the third category should proceed with a great deal of caution and are advised to begin by having a discussion with a mental health professional or their GP before assuming that childhood sexual abuse is at the root of their difficulties. If there are no clear memories, then it can be extremely difficult to *prove* that anything happened and it is very unwise to proceed on the basis that the memories will somehow be 'recovered' along the way.

There has been an ongoing debate about the validity of recovered memories and about a condition known as False Memory Syndrome (Merskey 1996; Gardner 2004). Some groups in this debate are convinced that memories recovered in therapy (or elsewhere) are false and are the result of leading questions and suggestions by unethical or unskilled therapists. Another group insists that disturbing memories can be repressed for many years and that it is not surprising that people going through therapy sometimes remember a lot more about their past. Of course, *proving* that what has been 'remembered' actually happened is a different thing altogether and when recovered memories are presented as evidence in a legal setting the situation can become very complex.

A reasonable 'middle ground' (Dobson and Prout 1998) is to assume that it is possible that some people in therapy, perhaps as the result of undue prompting by a therapist who has jumped to conclusions, will experience 'memories' that do not actually represent what really happened to them. It is also possible that some people in therapy may remember things that actually happened to them even though they had not been able to recall them over the course of many years. For the vast majority, therapy around childhood sexual abuse will focus on clearly remembered events and, as a general rule, it is wise only to proceed if the memories are clear and evident. Of course, it is possible to work on the difficulty of 'not knowing', but this is very different from trying to look for proof of something that you cannot remember.

The interaction between memory and emotion is also very complex and the developing research evidence continues to improve our knowledge. However, we do not know all there is to know about this relationship. Hence, it is best to proceed with caution if you are in any doubt.

How to use this book

Reading through this book should provide you with a firm foundation for going into therapy. I hope that it will also give you some strategies and ideas that will help you to get the most from therapy and from your life beyond therapy. Take your time and work through one chapter at a time and then stop and think about how what you have read applies to you. Then move on, making sure that you have a good grasp of what has gone before. By the end of the book you should have a good understanding of how your experiences have affected you as an individual and what you can do to start making positive changes. If you feel confused or unsure, then just go back and pick up the thread again. Try to resist rushing through the book or making snap decisions about therapy. Instead, it is better to take your time and to make sure that you are clear about what you want to achieve before you go ahead.

Your reactions to reading the book

Thinking, reading and talking about childhood sexual abuse is bound to be difficult for anyone. Because it can be unsettling to read about childhood sexual abuse, it is important to establish right at the start that if it becomes too upsetting then *stop!* Put the book down and go and do something else that you know will help you feel okay. It is not a sign of failure or weakness to accept that you are distressed – quite the opposite. Uncomfortable feelings will be stirred up. If and when this happens as you read through the book, try to notice how you feel and how that makes you want to react. If possible, write it down rather than acting on what you are feeling straight away. This will help you to begin to see how things link up, how particular thoughts and memories link to particular feelings and how those feelings link to how you behave as an individual.

If some of the things that you read about here remind you of specific things that happened to you, then your reaction is likely to be all the more powerful. For instance, you may notice some very sad feelings, or fear or anger building up. These might be difficult feelings to shake off straight away, so make sure that you put aside a time to read the book when you can relax and be free of interruptions and commitments. It is worth stating, as you go through the book, that you might become more irritable and short-tempered with the people around you, such as friends, family and colleagues. You might also notice more frequent dreams and nightmares. Some people might also experience 'flashbacks' or disturbing memories of the past that are so vivid that, just for a moment, it feels as if those things are actually happening again. Because of this you might also notice yourself doing *more* of the things that you usually do in order to try to stay calm, or 'self-soothe'. For instance, you might feel like drinking more alcohol, smoking more cigarettes, eating more comfort food or maybe even retreating to your bed.

If the methods you have relied on to settle yourself in the past are also 'self-destructive', then it is important to try to replace as many as you can with something more constructive along the way. For instance, throughout the book you will find frequent reminders and encouragement to write things down, to keep a diary or just to step back and reflect on what you are feeling. Of course, it is not easy to change habits just like that, but being prepared to give these new things a go and to give them time to help can make a big difference.

Considering 'change'

Of course, change is not easy. We all know it requires hard work and the willingness to experience pain and to explore aspects of oneself and one's past that are uncomfortable. Because of this it may also feel like an added injustice to have to go through this process when you are filled with a sense of having been so unfairly treated as a child. This is just one reason why 'change' can be so difficult to achieve and an example of why psychological therapy can be so challenging.

But because people *do* make important changes to the way that they think, feel and behave in therapy, it is also important to think about how change will affect you *and* those around you. Not only might you feel resistant to change, the people around you may be just as reluctant. None of us lives in a vacuum and when we change how we behave around others they are likely to notice and to react. Hopefully, the people you have in your life now will be positive and supportive; but this is not always the case. For example, imagine someone who comes away from therapy with more confidence, improved self-esteem and more sense of how they wish to be treated by others. If this puts strain on their relationship at home, then their partner may feel they have only two choices; either adapt to the changes or else resist and try to push things back to how they were. This kind of situation can quickly bring the issue of 'control' in relationships to the surface. If this has been a problem in the relationship before, then progress in therapy might begin to undermine an already unstable relationship, bringing things to a head. If it feels right and safe to do so, you might want to talk some of this through with, for example, your partner so that you work things through as they go along. However, if you don't feel safe to talk about these things, then try to bear in mind, as you go through the book, whether this aspect of your relationship will hinder your progress in the future and how you might address it if it becomes a bigger problem.

By looking at these issues in more depth, this book will help you to consider in advance how beneficial it is to 'set the stage' before going into therapy. For example, ask yourself right now how your friends and family would react if you really were to make the changes that you feel are necessary in your life. If you have a partner, how would they react if you were to become more assertive? How would your everyday life change if you were to take back some more of the control in close relationships? On the other hand, how would things change if you were to *let go* of some of the control you have been clinging to?

Below is a guide for professionals about how to use this book and when to suggest that people read it. Of course, if a professional has recommended the book to you, then talking it through with them is another good way to make sure that you get the most from it.

The next chapter provides a definition of childhood sexual abuse and is our starting point for getting an overview of the problem and its after-effects.

Guide for professionals

Using this book

This book is intended as a source of information and guidance for people who have experienced childhood sexual abuse. Having an explanation for some of one's difficulties can be a powerful intervention in its own right. The knowledge that difficulties in one's adult life can be reformulated as a 'normal reaction to abnormal circumstances' can also have profound and liberating effects. However, the relationship between childhood sexual abuse and difficulties in later life is often not straightforward. Clearly, some people who are seeking an 'explanation' for their difficulties may never have been abused, whereas others may well have been and have very clear memories of the facts. Therefore, it is recommended that these ideas should be discussed carefully with your client beforehand. This book should then be suggested when you and your client have established that childhood sexual abuse has been a very real issue for them and that it is continuing to have a major effect upon their well-being.

For people who are considering seeking psychological therapy, the book provides further information about some of the types of therapy that are generally available and that have also been shown to be effective in these circumstances. By providing clear guidelines for those seeking therapy, it is intended to help ensure that people find their way to a safe and effective source of help. Importantly, this book also emphasises the demands that engaging in psychological therapy makes upon the client. This information does not appear to have been generally available in the past. Being ill-prepared, misinformed and having unrealistic expectations are all impediments to progress in therapy. Likewise, having the motivation to pursue therapy and to work through the challenges is essential. Having sound information can promote motivation and encourage participation in the process of therapy. By preparing for therapy and by knowing more about what is available, people make informed choices and can help themselves to make the most of the therapy that is available to them.

One suggestion is to ask your client to read through the book and then arrange to meet with them again to talk things through in more depth before deciding on a course of action. This way you can both be sure that you are making the right choices.

Knowledge and evidence base

The knowledge and evidence base to the book has been drawn from longstanding and well-researched theories and practice alongside more contemporary research and comment. This is partly in order to demonstrate the consistent links between the early research and the work that is being conducted now. Research into the effects of childhood sexual abuse is always developing and new findings are always coming to the fore. So it is with the theory and practice of psychological therapy. The links at the back of the book will enable the interested professional to keep up to date.

2 Childhood sexual abuse: a definition and overview

The effects of childhood abuse are very broad ranging. They can also be extremely damaging and difficult to cope with. There is now an enormous amount of research evidence confirming the fact that childhood sexual abuse can profoundly affect child development (Hooper 1990; Ussher and Dewberry 1995). The difficulties can cover a wide range of areas, including:

- Physical well-being.
- Intellectual (or cognitive) functioning.
- Emotional health and stability.
- Social behaviour and relationships.

As individuals, we are a product of our biology and genetics, our personality and also the social influences we have around us. The ways in which these areas work together determine the kind of person we are, the way we relate to other people and how we get along in our everyday lives.

In this book we will concentrate on how childhood sexual abuse affects people emotionally and psychologically; in other words, how it affects the way they think, feel and behave. Of course, a huge range of other problems in our everyday lives can affect us too, but the foundations laid down in childhood can ultimately influence how these things affect us. For instance, imagine the person who has been brought up to feel that they are as good as other people. Imagine that their well-being and happiness has been nurtured and that they have been treated with respect and care. Someone with this kind of foundation is probably more likely to cope with the challenges of adult life than the person who has been abused, neglected and mistreated as a child. It is important to have good self-esteem and a sense of oneself as being valuable and worthwhile without having to *earn* the privilege in some way. If it is difficult to see the value in oneself then, at worst, it can become increasingly difficult to see the point in struggling with the challenges of everyday life. Depression is strongly linked to abuse in childhood (Kendler *et al.* 2004). It has also long been recognised that the incidence of suicide in those who have been abused as children is also disproportionately high (Bagley and Young 1990). The potential after-effects of sexual abuse cannot be considered lightly.

What is sexual abuse?

Because the range of sexual acts involved in childhood sexual abuse can be so broad and so varied, clear-cut definitions of what makes something abusive have been difficult to establish. In any case, it can be unhelpful to try to 'compare' one set of abusive experiences with another, since the details of any two individuals' lives are rarely so alike. Instead it is more useful to think about childhood sexual abuse across a broad spectrum with many different factors and issues to consider along the way. For example, for some people the abuse happens once and then stops, whereas for others it can happen repeatedly and over several years. It is common for violence or the threat of violence to be used, but for many the abuse may have involved emotional pressure or grooming through gifts and attention instead. It can also be important to consider whether others knew about the abuse at the time but seemed to do nothing to prevent it. Thinking about these issues is difficult and important because the type of situation, or context, in which the abuse occurred can have additional effects in terms of undermining trust and inducing fear and shame.

Case example – Sarah

Sarah's parents separated when she was 6 years old. She stayed with her mother and younger sister after her father left. After a number of temporary moves, Sarah's mother eventually found suitable rented accommodation and they settled down. The rent was slightly more than she could afford and so finances continued to be tight. Sarah was a bright child and did well at school once she had settled into the new area.

An older man in the same block of flats soon befriended her mum. He seemed nice enough and began to help out here and there, eventually offering to sit in with the children whilst her mum went out to one of her numerous part-time jobs. She was grateful for his help and he seemed to get on with the children. Sarah got on with him and he seemed interested in her schoolwork and in how she was getting on. Because he knew money was in short supply he sometimes gave Sarah some extra pocket money but told her not to tell her mum. One time, when he was babysitting and her sister had gone to bed, he sat closer to her and started to touch her in a way that did not feel right. Sarah felt very confused and did not know what to do. It happened again the next time and she protested, but he said he would tell her mum that she was 'naughty' and would stop coming round to help. He warned Sarah that her mum would not be able to keep things going if he was not around to help out and said that they would have to move again. Sarah felt trapped and did not say anything to her mum.

As in this example, the context surrounding the abuse itself can also be very important to consider. For Sarah, the additional sense of guilt at having accepted pocket money and her worries about having to move again could easily make the situation all the more confusing and distressing for her. The situational factors surrounding sexual abuse can all add up in a negative way, adding to the damaging effect of the abuse itself. Since the effects are so broad ranging, it is hard to imagine any childhood sexual abuse that is ever without consequence. Considering this, we can then begin to talk of 'abusive situations' as well as 'abusive acts'. This is important because it is not just the physical acts of abuse that have the lasting impact; it is also the personal and emotional damage that accompanies them that we must consider.

Sadly, some of the situations in which sexual abuse has been shown to be more likely tend to have multiple risk factors. For instance, childhood sexual abuse within a family is often (but not always) associated with other longstanding problems within the child's family. Physical and emotional neglect and a general lack of good parenting are often part of the background. This may be because the parents have themselves been the victims of inadequate or abusive parenting. Sometimes it is because they are struggling with other issues that mean that they are not able, or willing, to be available to look after their children. Of course, these factors do not *cause* child abuse, but they can certainly increase the overall risks and add to the difficulties that the child who experiences sexual abuse has to contend with.

To understand how an abusive act is likely to affect an individual, we need to consider other factors. For example:

- The age of the child at the time of the abuse.
- The child's developmental progress up to the time of the abuse.

- The age difference between the child and the perpetrator at the time of the abuse.
- The biological and/or social relationship between the child and the perpetrator.
- The nature and frequency of the sexually abusive acts.
- The way in which those acts were perpetrated. In other words, the degree to which the acts were unwanted, forced or endured under some degree of emotional pressure or threat.

To some degree 'abuse' is also defined according to local law and regional social mores. For instance, in the UK and in terms of consent to sexual activity, a child is any individual under the age of 16, but definitions of 'childhood' vary across cultures. Despite the difficulties with definitions, an essential starting point is for us to establish some basic concepts:

- Without question, *any* sexual act with a child is abusive.
- Children do *not* have the capacity to consent to a sexual relationship.

Of course, there are many different types of sexually abusive acts and behaviour. In recognising this, Mott defines sexual abuse as 'the sexual exploitation of a child for the sexual gratification of an adult' (2003). This type of definition leaves us in no doubt that, since sexual activity should only take place between consenting persons, and since children are unable to give consent, any sexual relationship with a child is abusive.

Different researchers have defined sexual abuse in different ways and their findings can vary as a result. For this reason, research that uses a broad and inclusive definition provides the best starting point. For example, Finkelhor and colleagues (1990, 1994) used a definition of abuse that included a wide range of sexual acts. Their definition included attempted and actual intercourse, oral or manual contact between a child and an adult, exhibitionism and photography of the child for sexual purposes. Research using this definition produced shocking statistics and the results have been replicated across the world.

At this point then we can say that the sexual abuse of a child involves:

- A sexual act (of which there is a very broad range of behaviours) which is designed to provide the adult perpetrator with sexual gratification.

- A child victim of these acts who is therefore not able, under *any* circumstances, to give appropriate consent.

There are no exceptions or 'special' circumstances in which these rules do not apply. It is extremely important to be clear about this essential point and to establish that the inclusion of children in any sexual act cannot be anything other than abusive.

Even within this basic definition, the variations and complications are infinite. A meaningful definition of abuse must therefore strive to take account of, for example, the impact of a one-off sexual remark by a stranger that made the child feel uncomfortable. But it must also be able to take account of incidents of repeated sexual intercourse over many years by a family member or an organised paedophile ring. Coercion, seduction, 'special' treatment, drugs and alcohol and threats or acts of violence may also accompany the sexual acts themselves. The perpetrator may try to trap the child by telling them that no-one will believe them or that they, or someone else, will get hurt if anyone finds out. They may provide rewards for taking part and keeping quiet and they may treat their victim as if they are special, they may even tell them what happens between them is a sign of the 'special' relationship they have together. These are just a few examples of the way in which the perpetrator can intensify or even try to disguise the basically abusive nature of their behaviour. By understanding these aspects as *part of the whole abusive experience*, it is easy to see that sexual abuse involves an exploitation of the child's mind, their feelings as well as their body. These factors change the way that children think and feel about themselves in profound and significant ways. They also sow the seeds for a range of potential difficulties in later life.

Research evidence

Like dropping a pebble into a pool, abuse has multiple after-effects. These may not be at all obvious at first sight. This is one reason why the research of the last three decades has been so important, since it has repeatedly demonstrated the links between sexually abusive events in childhood and difficulties in adult life. The existing research confirms the following:

- Childhood sexual abuse is not uncommon.
- There are certain social and situational risk factors that increase the likelihood of a child being abused.

- The experience of having been abused as a child can increase the risk of psychological and developmental difficulties in childhood and, likewise, can increase the risk of mental health problems in adult life.

How many people have been abused in childhood?

Research

For several reasons, it has been difficult to establish a straightforward figure for the number of people that have suffered sexual abuse as children. Thirty years ago this was partly because society at large had not recognised nor accepted that sexual abuse was occurring on the scale that researchers were beginning to report. Once this disturbing fact had been acknowledged, researchers continued to struggle to paint a clear picture. This was less because of denial or disbelief, but more because of the difficulties in measuring something so broad, varied and widespread.

Research of this kind also depends heavily on finding a representative sample group around whom conclusions about the general population can be based. This can be complicated, especially when considering an emotive issue such as childhood sexual abuse. People who have experienced abuse in childhood may be understandably reluctant to share their experiences, especially in a research setting. This is one of the reasons why most researchers conclude that, despite any figures they generate, the extent of sexual abuse in childhood is most probably grossly under-reported (Peters *et al.* 1986). A general estimate is that less than 50 per cent of cases of childhood sexual abuse are actually reported (Ussher and Dewberry 1995; Oaksford and Frude 2001).

How widespread is the problem?

In an attempt to get an accurate picture, researchers begin by agreeing a definition of abuse for the purposes of their study. A representative sample is then selected in order to establish 'prevalence'. Prevalence is an estimate of the number of people in the population at large who could be said to be suffering from a particular condition, at any one time. This is often reported as a proportion of a given number of people or as a percentage (e.g. 3 people per 1000 or 0.3 per cent of the adult population).

This kind of information (known as epidemiology) is extremely useful because it allows us to begin to see the scale of a particular problem. Ideally, this means that the necessary resources can eventually be put into place to provide appropriate support. It also increases the chances for effective preventative measures to be worked out. For instance, we might hope that by raising the profile of a particular condition and promoting public awareness, changes can also be made at a societal level.

In reviewing some of the research related to the incidence and prevalence of childhood sexual abuse, a particular picture emerges. For example, Peters and colleagues (1986) looked at 19 research projects conducted in the USA between 1929 and 1985. They reported a large variation in the findings in terms of how many adults reported having been sexually abused in childhood. The figures were between 6 per cent and 62 per cent for females and between 3 per cent and 31 per cent for males. However, an average of the studies listed provided figures more like 23 per cent for females and 10 per cent for males. Even the lower estimates indicate an extremely serious problem that affects enormous numbers of people; the higher figures suggest an ongoing problem of truly epidemic proportions!

Based on a similar overview of US and European studies published between 1990 and 1996, Fergusson and Mullen (1999) also recognised that estimates of prevalence vary greatly, partly because of the broad range of definitions of abuse that researchers use. For example, using a broad definition that included non-contact sexual acts, figures were as high as 62 per cent for females and 29 per cent for males. When the definition of abuse was restricted to attempted and actual penetrative sexual acts, this figure was more like 28 per cent for females and 14 per cent for males. Most studies in this sample found that between 15 per cent and 30 per cent of females and between 3 per cent and 15 per cent of males had been exposed to some form of sexual abuse as children. Fergusson and Mullen also concluded that there was consistent evidence to indicate that between 5 per cent and 10 per cent of children in the general population have been exposed to *severely abusive* acts involving attempted or actual penetration. Furthermore, in relation to the more severe forms of abuse, there seemed to be little difference between males and females in terms of prevalence.

A study of prevalence in Great Britain (Baker and Duncan 1985) sampled over 2000 men and women. Ten per cent reported they had been abused before the age of 16. This broke down into 12 per cent of females and 8 per cent of males. If we apply these average figures to current UK population estimates, then an astonishing picture emerges. The UK currently has a population of just over 60 million people, 80 per cent of whom are over the age of 16 (National Statistics 2007). Applying Baker and Duncan's findings suggests that approximately 5 million UK adults have suffered some kind of sexual abuse as children. That is 3 million women and 2 million men. When we consider that the current adult population of London is currently around 6 million, then it is possible to begin to imagine the scale of the problem. In short, the prevalence of sexual abuse in the UK alone is truly staggering. Clearly, there is a dire need to continually repeat this kind of research. Perhaps unsurprisingly, these findings echo those of many others in other parts of the world (Finkelhor 1994). With these observations in mind, it is clear that not only has the sexual abuse of children been an enormous and enduring problem, but it appears to be continuing at a very high rate.

By pulling some of the major pieces of research together, some general trends have emerged. By following those leads, for example by looking for patterns within families and the characteristics of those children who have reported abuse, particular risk factors can be seen. These factors will be discussed again in chapter 2, when we look more closely at families and the context in which children grow up, but some general points to consider are as follows:

- Children of both sexes are at risk of sexual abuse.
- Approximately 10 per cent of children will be exposed to some kind of sexual abuse before adulthood; however, it is widely acknowledged that this is likely to be an underestimate.
- Around 50 per cent of the abuse that occurs involves physical contact.
- Girls are approximately twice as likely to be abused as boys.
- Overall, children are especially at risk between the ages of 4 and 12 years.
- Girls are at greatest risk between the ages of 10 and 12 years.
- Approximately 50 per cent of abusers are known to the children they abuse.
- Girls appear to be more likely to be abused by someone in their immediate family.
- Overall, girls also appear to be at slightly greater risk of abuse from strangers than boys.
- Boys are at greater risk of being abused by someone known to them, but *outside* the family, such as a neighbour or an authority figure of some kind.

- Just over half of the incidents of sexual abuse appear to be single events, but approximately 25 per cent of those who have been abused were abused repeatedly.
- Girls appear to be at slightly greater risk of being abused by more than one person over time.
- An 'unhappy family life' is linked with higher rates of sexual abuse.
- Separation from one or both biological parents for a major part of one's life is associated with higher rates of sexual abuse.
- Poor sex education has been linked to higher rates of sexual abuse.
- Less than 50 per cent of those who have suffered abuse are likely to disclose what has happened to them.

Subjective reports of the damage caused by childhood sexual abuse suggest that it is more severe in women who have been abused repeatedly within the family and in which the abuse began before the age of 10 years. However, this is perhaps just one example of a particularly damaging combination of circumstances.

3   The impact of childhood sexual abuse upon the individual

The initial effects of childhood sexual abuse

This issue will be explored more fully in Part II, but, for now, there are some general points to bear in mind. For instance, the immediate impact of sexual abuse upon children is often both severe and profound. It is also widely accepted that children experience abuse as frightening, painful, disturbing and psychologically damaging. Added to this, as we have seen already, there are a whole range factors to consider concerning the 'context' and nature of the abuse that can also influence the particular effects it can have.

Historically, research into the effects of childhood sexual abuse has tended to focus on the long-term effects as found in adults. However, it is equally important to understand the immediate effects abuse can have upon children as they are growing up. At the same time, it is encouraging to note that there is significant evidence to suggest that children who receive therapeutic input at an early stage are able to benefit from it (Fergusson and Mullen 1999, 61; Hetzel et al. 2007).

The details will vary depending upon the age and developmental stage of the child when the abuse occurs, but immediate effects can be summarised in terms of a broad range of behavioural, emotional and social difficulties. Behavioural symptoms might include bed-wetting, soiling or even some kind of self-harm. Emotional reactions such as anxiety, depression or withdrawal from others are also not uncommon. Children who are being abused can often show signs of disturbed social relationships with friends and peers such as withdrawal, overly sexualised behaviour and aggression.

There are some other general characteristics that can indicate that there is a problem. These sometimes appear in the form of 'accommodation syndrome' (Summit 1983). The main signs of this are secrecy, helplessness, passivity, delayed disclosure and retraction. We can appreciate that this may well be what happens when a child is in an impossible and disturbing situation. As such, 'accommodating' can be seen as a form of 'playing dead'. For instance, a child who has been told that they will be punished or hurt if they tell anyone what is going on will quickly learn that the 'best' thing to do is to keep quiet, offer no resistance and keep on hoping that something will change without them having to disclose the situation themselves. From the outside this apparently 'passive' attitude may make it appear as if the child is somehow giving consent, or else is not disturbed by what is going on. Of course, the opposite is true and this is one of the distortions of truth perpetrators may rely upon to justify their own behaviour. The psychological and emotional pressure upon children who are being abused can be enormous. For instance, when a child is deliberately encouraged to believe that the person abusing them will go to prison and that their family will then disintegrate, they are unlikely to speak out. Similarly, if a child believes that by not pro-testing they are protecting their mother or their siblings from further abuse, then there is also tremendous pressure upon them not to resist.

Of course, it is this level of gross mistreatment and exploitation of the child's vulnerability, dependency and powerlessness in relation to the adult that is emotionally 'abusive' over and above any sexual act that may be involved. This emphasises again the point that the sexual abuse of children is clearly an abuse of both body *and* mind.

The results of this kind of stress will almost certainly show up elsewhere in some of the characteristic ways already mentioned. It is also not surprising that a child experiencing this kind of disturbing situation will 'act out' or display their distress in some noticeable way. One example is by misbehaving more at school or by changing their behaviour in such away that others might notice. For instance, an ordinarily placid child may suddenly become more aggressive and disruptive at home. Hopefully, as the social climate becomes more informed and aware of the problem of sexual abuse, these signs will be picked up more quickly.

Case example – Anna

When Anna was 10 years old, her stepfather began to come into her room at night and sexually abuse her. He was a drinker and after a night in the pub he would sometimes come straight into her room on his return. When this happened he was always drunk and smelt strongly of cigarette smoke, alcohol and sweat. Anna quickly began to dread the turn of the key in the door, believing that he was on his way to her room.

More often than not he walked straight past, but she never knew she was okay until she heard him getting into his own bed and falling asleep.

When he abused her, he would hold her down and put his hand across her mouth or push her face into a pillow. This meant she could not call out, even if she was brave enough to do so, but since he used so much force she often felt as though she was about to pass out. On several occasions she believed she would die if he did not take his hand away soon.

After a few months Anna told her mother that her stepfather was coming into her room and 'doing things' to her. Her mother did not appear to believe her and angrily told her off for being so rude before sending her to her bedroom. That night Anna overheard a blazing row downstairs. The abuse stopped there and then. After two or three more years her stepfather left. Anna's mother said it was because he was having an affair with another woman.

Anna did not manage the move to secondary school very well. She had been an outgoing and able child at junior school. She was anxious and rarely took part in what was going on around her. Anna had one or two close friends who also seemed quite withdrawn and lacking in confidence. Anna became easy to overlook because she hid herself away so well at school.

In this example, the changes in Anna's behaviour were more difficult to spot because of the other changes going on in her life. So, whilst the signs that something was wrong were there, it would not have been easy, even for someone who knew her well, to have put the pieces together. Of course, as Anna became more withdrawn, the opportunities for her to reach out to other people, and vice versa, would be likely to become increasingly few and far between.

A useful model and framework

The researchers David Finkelhor and Angela Browne (1986) devised a model to help understand and explain the effects of childhood sexual abuse. We will spend more time on this model in Part II of the book, but it is useful to have an understanding of these ideas now. The model highlights four main aspects of childhood sexual abuse, which are referred to as 'traumagenic dynamics'. These are:

- sexual traumatisation
- betrayal

- stigmatisation
- powerlessness.

Pinpointing these important areas can help us to further recognise that sexual abuse is not only a physically traumatic abuse of the child's body, it is also a major betrayal of the child's trust in the belief that adults are there to protect them. As a result, sexual abuse undermines the child's trust in others in an extremely damaging way. Sexual abuse also marks children out as 'different' in a way that leads them to feel stigmatised and marked out from others by their experiences. For instance, they might feel as if they themselves are 'dirty' or as if they are 'damaged goods'. The sense of shame that can follow on from this is often a real problem that can endure well into adulthood. This model also reminds us that sexual abuse involves an exploitation of the child's powerlessness – often in relation to an older, stronger, more sophisticated and more powerful person in their lives. This can further undermine the child's trust that others will behave well and not exploit them, and makes their withdrawal and anxiety an understandable reaction.

With these issues in mind, it is very likely that there will be significant knock-on effects upon the child's development that will create problems for them in the future.

The long-term impact upon adults

There is also a significant amount of evidence to indicate that the after-effects of abuse can greatly increase the risk of psychological and emotional difficulties in adulthood. Contrary to popular belief, there is evidence to suggest that the after-effects can actually become more difficult with age (Baker and Duncan 1985). One explanation of this is that an individual's perception of the negative impact of abuse in childhood can actually increase over time, perhaps as the result of greater hindsight and life experience. Of course, it would be very important to discover whether this can be reversed if more adults were to enter into effective therapy. So far, there are encouraging suggestions that good early intervention can protect against this effect (Finkelhor and Berliner 1995).

Once again, these ideas will be explored further in Part III, but for now there are some general conclusions to consider. Over the last two decades researchers have compared adults who have experienced abuse as children with the population as a whole. These results consistently link childhood sexual abuse with an increased risk of going on to suffer from one, or more, of the following:

- anxiety disorders
- depressive disorders
- Post-Traumatic Stress Disorder
- self-harm and suicide
- eating disorders
- substance misuse
- relationship difficulties
- personality disorders.

Of course, there are many other factors in both childhood and adulthood that can also increase the risk of developing these kinds of difficulties. Nevertheless, the research available so far appears to establish that a history of childhood abuse can significantly increase the risk of psychological and developmental difficulties in childhood and, likewise, can increase the risk of mental health problems in adult life.

Multiple difficulties and vicious circles

Beyond the statistics, it is important to think about how these issues might affect each individual. One aspect of the effects of childhood sexual abuse that can be missed when researchers takes a 'snapshot' of the population are the long-term problems that can build up over time. For example, someone who suffered sexual abuse as a child may begin adulthood with a range of difficulties. Further obstacles and challenges in that person's life can then just serve to add to their troubles.

Case example – Mark

Mark's mother sexually abused him from the age of 8 until he was about 12. His father had apparently not known what was going on. As Mark found out more about sex and healthy sexual relationships at school and from his friends, he realised that what was happening at home was not 'okay' as his mother had told him. By angrily protesting and threatening to tell his father, he managed to bring the abuse to an end, but the relationship with his mother soon took another nasty turn. He quickly fell from 'favour' and increasingly found himself on the receiving end of his mother's temper instead. Naturally, this was very difficult for him to deal with, but he preferred this to what had gone before, and realised he just had to bide his time before he could leave.

Mark left home at 15 after dropping out of school. Although others thought he would do well, Mark began to lose interest in anything other than just getting away. His behaviour was occasionally disruptive and challenging, but not that different to many other boys of his age. Consequently, his teachers did not guess what was going on, especially because Mark kept his feelings to himself at school and was good at hiding behind his bravado and quick wit. After moving out of the family home, he slept on various friends' sofas, but soon felt he had outstayed his welcome and quickly moved on.

Partly because of the uncertainty and the emptiness of his everyday life, Mark sought an escape in smoking cannabis. He sometimes used other drugs when he could get hold of them. He managed like this for several years. Mark learned how to get along with people in order to get a roof over his head, although things never stayed settled for long. He drifted from one job to another and found it difficult to get on with his bosses. Mark took criticism badly and often reacted angrily and aggressively. He told himself he would never let anyone treat him badly again and was always ready to stand up for himself.

In the example above, Mark sets out to escape the difficulties at home. In many ways, he was probably far from ready to move on and that left him vulnerable. His sense of self-esteem was low and he struggled just to get the basics in place. Of course, this did not give him a good platform upon which to build a life for himself. His troubles soon stacked up and included housing problems, drug misuse, instability and generally poor prospects. In time we would imagine that this would begin to take a toll on his physical health. On top of this, he is likely to still be carrying the emotional scars of the abuse and to continue to have a poor sense of what he has to offer. He is likely to continue to find trust particularly difficult and he may believe that by staying 'light-footed' and moving on, he can stay out of trouble. Of course, this means that his life may never have the chance to take shape. From this brief, but all too common example, it is easy to imagine the many ways in which the foundations of early childhood can either help, or profoundly hinder, one's ability to deal with adult life without it becoming a battleground.

Undoing the influence of the past upon the present

Once we recognise that childhood experiences can shape our adult life, we can start to do something about it in the here-and-now. Remembering the past and exploring the beliefs that were generated about ourselves in childhood means we can begin to sort through what we need to keep and what really belongs in the past. By gradually understanding the impact of the past upon the present, it becomes possible to undo the influence of destructive past experiences.

Sexual abuse in childhood can have a broad range of effects upon the way we think, feel and behave as adults. It can also affect the kinds of relationships we have with those around us. Because feelings of frustration, fear and shame can be so powerful, the person who has experienced sexual abuse can also be left with a range of emotional difficulties, including mood disorders such as anxiety and depression. But sometimes attempts to treat 'symptoms' alone can fail to recognise that they are the outward signs of more underlying troubles.

As well as providing information about the effects of sexual abuse, this book is intended as an invitation to take the time to think about the connections between past and present in your own life. If you are someone who is considering therapy but are unsure as to which way to go, this may make those difficult conversations, perhaps with a partner or with a professional, a little easier. It will also help you to give yourself realistic expectations about how things might improve. For instance, you may decide to enter more long-term therapy rather than choosing something that helps you with the symptoms, such as anxiety, alone. Of course, this means being realistic about the added challenge that this can involve. Whichever route you choose, engaging in therapy can feel like a leap of faith and this book is intended to help make that leap less daunting.

How do you cope now?

People find different ways to cope with difficult feelings and experiences. Some of these 'coping mechanisms' are better for us than others. When we are in distress we all try to find ways to feel better, if only for a little while. Of course, some of these methods can just create more problems. For example, some people turn to drugs or alcohol, whilst others seem to dash from one doomed but exciting relationship to another. By contrast, some people only really feel comfortable when they have withdrawn from the world into the safety of their own home. However, the more we come to rely on particular ways of coping, the more of a *habit* they can become.

Habits are difficult to change. Also they usually only provide temporary relief from negative feelings. If this is the case, it may seem to you that there is little time to stand back and really come to terms with what is going on in the background. Sometimes, in a busy life, it is easy to feel as though there is little opportunity to step off the tread-mill of endlessly repeating patterns of thoughts, feelings and beha-viour. These 'patterns', as we shall see, can cut across many areas of one's everyday life and can affect many of the experiences we have as adults. Because of this, the damage caused by childhood sexual abuse can carry on making it difficult to really engage in life in a more positive and rewarding way. Therapy can be about spotting these patterns and learning new ways to cope with difficult memories and uncomfortable feelings so that you get a chance to step off the treadmill.

Of course, people have a wide variety of beliefs about why we are the way we are. For instance, many people believe that their way of doing things is somehow 'etched in stone' since they were simply 'born' that way. People with this view of the world will probably see little point in trying to change. They might also see their personal characteristics, their frequent periods of depression, their disturbed sleep and their difficulties with all kinds of close relationships as just something else they were born with. Of course, the risk here is that these characteristics become part and parcel of their sense of identity.

What follows over the next few chapters is a different way of looking at things. It is a way of understanding how childhood abuse can lay the foundations for certain negative patterns of behaviour, thoughts and feelings in adulthood. If we accept that anyone who has been abused or mistreated as a child is likely to develop certain symptoms and difficulties in adult life, then it is possible to start to separate the sense of oneself as an individual from one's symptoms and difficulties. It might then be easier to accept that people are not necessarily 'bad' even though 'bad' things have happened to them as children.

Hopefully it then becomes easier to see your symptoms less as the result of some character flaw, and more as the result of having suffered extreme and painful experiences when you were least able to cope with them. By considering the idea that your symptoms could be seen as normal reactions to abnormal and traumatic events in child-hood, it is possible to usher in the idea of *change*. Then there may be more room for some compassion towards yourself as someone who perhaps had no choice but to try and survive – as best as possible – with the limited resources available to you in childhood.

4 Beyond the individual: child sexual abuse and society

Childhood sexual abuse and the general population

As discussed earlier, research into the nature and extent of childhood sexual abuse has had a difficult beginning and does not have an especially long pedigree compared to many other areas of social research. Firstly, there may well have been great resistance to the shocking picture that early studies began to reveal. Secondly, the methods used to gather information have varied in quality and this has made it difficult to compare findings across studies and across different populations. It is equally difficult to attempt reliable comparisons across time, although these methods are constantly being refined.

Despite the limitations, the profile of childhood sexual abuse has certainly been raised within the public eye, especially over the last 20 years or so. National campaigns and the development of services such as Childline have been matched by concerted efforts in terms of raising professional awareness of child protection issues. For many working with children and families, this has involved training in spotting the signs of distress and maltreatment in children who may be being abused. Of course, the system is not foolproof, and if we are to reduce the numbers described earlier there is clearly an immense amount of work yet to do.

One effect of the campaign to raise awareness of child sexual abuse in the public consciousness has been to make it appear as if it is increasing. Of course, it may also be that, as a society, we are simply talking about it more and being more open about the reality of its occurrence.

In the same way, because the research methods have improved since the very early studies, the number of cases may appear to have increased. This is not necessarily because there are *more* cases to report, but could be because the researchers are asking the types of questions that make it more likely for them to get more accurate results. As more people become aware of the realities and effects of sexual abuse, it might also be the case that they feel more inclined to speak out and contribute to raising the profile of this enormous problem. Taken together, this may make it look as if the numbers are going up. At this stage it is, unfortunately, impossible to say which is the case. However, the next wave of research may need to be specifically aimed at looking at this issue so that we are in a better position to comment on trends and patterns and how they reflect reality.

Changes over time?

Because consistently good quality research into childhood sexual abuse has only been available relatively recently, little work has been done on measuring changes over time. However, Wyatt and colleagues (1999), in an American study, set out to measure changes in the amount of child sexual abuse that took place over a single decade. Using the same method as in an earlier study (Wyatt 1985), the team interviewed over 300 African and European American women. They found over one third reported at least one incident of sexual abuse before the age of 18. This had not changed significantly since 1984, when slightly more of the population sample interviewed reported having been abused. Their figure, of approximately one third of the population, when using a broad definition of abuse, is one that seems to hold across many studies. They also found a tendency towards more single acts of abuse rather than repeated acts. However, in the follow-up study, the team found an increase in the reporting of more severe forms of abuse (including penetrative sexual acts). There was also some indication that the average age of perpetrators had changed, with more being under the age of 25 in the later study. The most notable aspect of this piece of work is the similarity of the results across time and in relation to a host of other studies.

Childhood sexual abuse and the media

There are, of course, many issues to consider in relation to the way that childhood sexual abuse is portrayed in the media. For instance, high-profile cases are often sensationalised. Unfortunately, this can obscure the ongoing struggle of many others who are dealing with the everyday reality of sexual abuse. Public appreciation of the long-term effects and the day-to-day struggle to have a 'normal' life once the abuse has stopped often appear to take second place to modifying legislation, seeing justice done and apportioning blame. This can conceal the fact that the sexual abuse of children is taking place day after day across the world, and that the vast majority of cases will never receive public attention.

On the other hand, not publicising the issue would risk returning to an age where the occurrence of abuse is not discussed, drawing an equally unhelpful veil of silence over it once again.

Clearly these issues need to be considered in parallel, and it is of the utmost importance to keep the debate alive whilst trying to tread a line between sensationalism on one hand and complacency on the other.

Disclosure – the difficult problem of letting people know

Researchers found that around 50 per cent of those interviewed as adults had not disclosed what had happened to them as children at the time it occurred (Finkelhor *et al.* 1990; Ussher and Dewberry 1995). Some later studies have suggested that this figure has remained about the same over time (Wyatt *et al.* 1999), whilst others (Fergusson and Mullen 1999) suggest that disclosure rates are slowly increasing.

This would be encouraging, given the concerted attempts to raise public awareness and to publicise the problem of all kinds of child abuse around the world. One possible benefit of this publicity is that it may help to lift the burden of shame from those who have experienced abuse as children and prompt them to share what has happened with others they can trust.

Are different groups affected in different ways?

Some thought has been given to the idea that different time periods and events on the world stage may give rise to changes in the incidence of childhood sexual abuse. Once again, we are restricted by research that only allows us to look back over the last few decades. Nevertheless, researchers such as Russell (1986) have begun to explore the presence of so-called 'cohort effects', suggesting that groups in different periods of time have been at varying levels of risk. One example is that children in the period of the Second World War were at greater risk, possibly because there were so many changes in family life at the time (Finkelhor *et al.* 1990). For instance, it is easy to imagine that risk factors, such as separation from one's biological father, would have been much more pronounced.

If the great strides made by the major health, educational and welfare institutions in the last few years have really had an effect, then this should begin to show up in future cohort effects. As the evidence base provided by good-quality research continues to build up, it is not unreasonable to assume that this kind of comparative information should be available to us in the not-too-distant future. On the basis of that, we may be able to conclude with confidence that prolonged awareness-raising efforts have indeed been of benefit to more recent generations of children.

How does the problem vary across the world?

It has been difficult to make detailed comparisons across countries and cultures, mainly because there are so many obstacles to overcome in terms of variations in the methods used by researchers. However, from the available information it is possible to establish that the sexual abuse of children is clearly an international problem. For example, in one study Finkelhor (1994) analysed around 20 research papers in order to make some initial comments about international rates of abuse. Despite the variability in the quality of the studies, he reported rates of between 7 per cent and 36 per cent for women and between 3 per cent and 29 per cent for men. Once again, girls appeared to be between 1.5 and 3 times more likely than boys to experience sexual abuse in childhood. Across the studies, approximately 50 per cent of those taking part had also not disclosed the abuse at the time. All of the studies found a link between a history of sexual abuse and adult mental health difficulties, and as the quality of the research methods improved, so the number of cases increased.

A continual problem for society

Clearly the sexual abuse of children has a long history and has emerged as an international problem of epidemic proportions. What does this mean for us as a society? Firstly, the persistence of the problem would suggest that efforts to reduce it have so far been less successful than had been initially hoped. Whilst it is early days for really understanding the effect of increased child protection policies and awareness-raising, it is of great concern that the effect has not been more pronounced. One interpretation is that these strategies are indeed gaining a foothold, but that we have simply been unaware of the true extent of the problem. While some high-profile cases appear to have an impact for a while, it is the everyday occurrence of sexual abuse that is perhaps the most insidious and most elusive aspect of this type of crime. If the child is too frightened to speak and is in the grip of the 'accommodation syndrome', described earlier, then there may be few outward signs that anything is wrong. It may only be the diligence and attention of parents, teachers and others combined with the confidence to raise such contentious concerns that makes the difference.

Review and exercise

Instead of carrying on with reading Part II, try stopping for a while and taking some time to think about what you have read. Take a moment to ask yourself if you have really understood what has been covered so far. If you are in any doubt, slow down, go back and read it through again.

Perhaps there were sections of Part I that you skipped, either because they did not seem relevant or because you did not really want to read them for one reason or another. Other sections may have held your attention more keenly and this may have stirred up all sorts of different feelings. For instance, reading about the immediate impact of sexual abuse on children may have triggered strong feelings. Perhaps it is uncomfortable to look back and recognise some of the signs and symptoms that you experienced as a child, especially if you feel those around you did not understood what was going on for you.

If you can, and if it feels safe to do so, it may be useful just to allow these feelings to surface for a while rather than trying to get away from them too quickly. In order to help you deal with them safely you may well find that having a notebook or a personal journal of some kind will be especially useful for you at this point. For instance, you can use it to note down thoughts and memories that may be triggered off as you read, but which then disappear beneath the surface, just like dreams. At a later date, looking back over the kinds of things that come up at different times can also be a great source of reassurance that things *are* changing for you even though the process can seem like heavy going.

To get you started try this exercise. Take a piece of paper and write down one or two of the first words that spring to mind. Of course, there are no right or wrong answers, but just try to notice what happens and what words come up. Once you have some words on paper, read on.

Now, have a think about the following questions:

- Did you write one word, or none, or did you want to keep on writing?
- What will you do with the piece of paper now you have written these words on it?
- What *feelings* do you have right now about the words you have written down?
- What do you believe the words you have written mean about you as a person?

This is not a test; it is simply to encourage you to spend some time noticing how thinking about this subject affects you. We all want to avoid pain, it is a basic human instinct, and reading this book and thinking about your past, especially if this was coloured by fear and distress, is not going to be easy. However, if you can learn to step back from yourself and notice how you have reacted to what you have read, this will be a helpful strategy as you carry on through the book.

In Part II we will explore the all-important process of child development in more detail.

Part II

Childhood sexual abuse and child development

5 An introduction to child development

Child development and adult personality

In order to understand the effects of childhood sexual abuse, it is important to have an overview of the way in which children grow and develop. In this chapter we will consider some of the basic ingredients of good childcare and highlight the important milestones associated with each stage of childhood. By looking at what children need in order to thrive and grow, we will then be able to identify some of the more damaging ways in which sexual abuse in childhood can lead to developmental problems. In Part III of this book, some of the ways in which these early difficulties can carry over into adulthood will also be explored in more detail.

Of course, childhood is an incredibly active period of growth and development. If we begin to imagine the sheer amount of change going on at every level, then the achievement of each and every individual is awe-inspiring. Whilst the child's body undertakes the marathon task of physical growth and development, their psychological and emotional development shifts through periods of massive reorganisation at the same time. For instance, if we imagine what is accomplished in the baby's first two years of life, then we can begin to appreciate that just the very business of sensing, communicating, moving around and developing the first impressions of a sense of 'self' are phenomenal tasks in their own right.

Then try to 'fast-forward' through time and consider the teenager struggling with their conflicting needs for security on the one hand and independence on the other. Added to this are the day-to-day difficulties of handling friendships, dealing with rivalries and competition, and taking first steps in intimacy. Of course, on top of this there is the business of finding a place in the world of work and setting one's sights on the future. Taken together, which is how it happens in real life, the situation seems so complex that it is easy to feel overwhelmed on their behalf.

Step forward in time once again to consider the adult in middle age, struggling with the competing demands and responsibilities of home, family, work, friends, ambition and personal fulfilment. Should they lose their own parents at some point during this stage, as many do, then they may also have to face an unwelcome recognition of their own mortality and vulnerability. Move forward in time once again and consider the older adult facing retirement. Perhaps having worked for several decades and raising children along the way, they now suddenly have time on their hands. The stresses and strains of the workaday world may have cast shadows upon their health and vitality but, as in every other 'stage' of life, they face yet another series of challenges. For instance, how do they begin to embrace this chapter of their lives; will they manage to look back over their experiences with a sense of satisfaction that will carry them forwards with purpose and self-acceptance? If they have not achieved a sense of satisfaction, will they look back only with resentment and regret?

This whistle-stop tour from birth to death is intended to underline the idea that development does not stop once we reach adulthood. Instead, it is a continuous process for all of us. Just as in every other aspect of the natural world, we (and our families) are always at some point in an ongoing life cycle. We are always moving forwards through one phase after another. With this in mind, it is essential that firm foundations, beginning in the womb, set the scene for later stages of development. In general, the better these foundations the more likely we are to fare well at each later stage. Of course, a good beginning does not *guarantee* that everything will turn out fine, but having firm foundations can only help when it comes to tackling the next hurdle.

If a good start in life continues to be an asset throughout one's adult life, then it follows that the reverse can be equally true. Early difficulties may well be expected to affect the ease with which the person tackles the next stage of life, and so on across the life cycle. Of course, none of us grows up in a vacuum and changes in one area of our lives are bound to have some effect in others. In many ways, the development of each individual can be thought of as an oceanic tide with the waves constantly moving forward through time with a relentless momentum. Each wave moves forward across a broad front, with the surge of each wave carrying huge amounts of water forwards both above and below the surface with tremendous force. Naturally, just as with the ocean's tides, obstacles can get in the way and break up the rolling edge of the waves. The shape of the seabed beneath can also shift and contort the mass of water flowing around it, causing undercurrents and awkward crosscurrents. These currents might not be visible on the surface, but they will certainly be felt by anyone caught up in their wake.

If we use this image to think about personal development, then we can see that obstacles are always present by way of life's unpredictable ups and downs. Nevertheless, we can also assume that the fewer obstructions there are to the forward flow of early development, the better.

Some useful models of child development

Over the years many different theories have been put forward to describe the process of human development. Because there are so many aspects to consider, it is easy to get caught up in one particular area or another. It will be more useful at this point to take a holistic approach that allows us to think about child development in a more comprehensive way.

The models presented in this book are intended to provide a framework that will help you to appreciate how the many different aspects of child development link up and influence each other over time. These ideas also come from a variety of sources, including child and adult psychologists and child development researchers. For instance, the work of Erik Erikson provides a map of human development that spans the entire life cycle from birth to death (Erikson 1950, 1959). Erikson's model marks out the typical human life span in terms of some of the major achievements that are essential to each stage.

The abilities to think, learn and remember are all essential tasks of childhood. This is referred to as 'cognitive development'. Children's cognitive skills go through several major stages as they progress through infancy and childhood and into adolescence. These are explored along with an introduction to the idea of 'schema' development. Schemas are the mental maps that we build up over the years and carry around with us in the way that we see ourselves and other people. These schemas can be helpful (adaptive) or unhelpful (maladaptive). Events in childhood can shape the schema that we take with us into adulthood. Understanding this link will help you when it comes to understanding how psychological therapy, especially Cognitive Behavioural Therapy (CBT), works.

Attachment Theory provides another particularly useful overview. This theory, attributed to John Bowlby (1988), clearly describes the central role of *relationships* in human development. Healthy and reliable relationships in one's early life are essential in providing firm foundations for later life. Having a sense that the important people in your life will be there for you and will not harm or abandon you is the cornerstone of feeling safe and secure. Mary Ainsworth, a renowned developmental psychologist and researcher, introduced the concept of a 'secure base' (Ainsworth *et al.* 1978) to describe this. Bowlby, a psychoanalyst, developed the idea in his extensive works on the subject. Because of the straightforward way in which this theory describes particular patterns of relationships between the child and the parent, we can use it to see how early patterns of relationships with one's parent can influence each subsequent stage of development.

We can use these ideas alongside each other to really begin to understand the extent of the influence of the past upon the present. Later, in Part IV, we will look at how different types of psychological therapy can be useful in helping to address some of the more destructive and unhelpful patterns of thinking, feeling and behaving that may have their roots in childhood. If these destructive patterns are the result of abuse or are the after-effects of the types of chaotic or neglectful situations in which abuse more usually occurs, then it is all the more important to appreciate how one's past continues to shape one's present. Taking the time to consider how these ideas might apply in your own life can provide an important first step in thinking about the role of psychological therapy. By doing so, you will be beginning to see the connections between the there-and-then and the here-and-now.

6 Models of child development

In this chapter we will explore some important models of child development. Of course, there are a great many elements to child development. These include the many physical, cognitive, emotional and social aspects both of the child's individual makeup and the world around them. The various influences on development can also be both 'positive' and 'negative'. It can be useful to think of child development as taking place within a 'context' that is always influenced by 'biology', 'psychology' and by the 'social' aspects of the child's world. This is sometimes referred to as a 'bio/psycho/social' approach and is a way of highlighting the impact of the many possible interactions between these major influences on the individual over the course of their lives.

Biological influences

These include 'genetic' factors as well as difficulties 'acquired' through illness and injury. For example, Down's syndrome is a genetic condition and is present from conception, whereas physical problems following an accident are acquired. Depending on the nature of the condition, biological factors can have an enormous effect on development. For instance, profound learning difficulties can be the result of the child's genetic makeup. Severe learning difficulties can be a very dominant force in terms of further development and can affect cognitive, emotional and social progress in fundamental ways. Of course, a loving and supportive family and appropriate physical and educational support can help to make sure that everyone reaches their potential, despite other limitations. Nevertheless, the nature and severity of any physical or biological conditions can clearly have a big influence on life-long development.

Psychological influences

These include general intelligence, language development and the ability to 'process' information using memory and imagination. The development of identity and a sense of oneself as an individual is also 'work in progress' throughout childhood and beyond. Of course, this involves the development of one's sexual identity, morality and spirituality along with the many other highly individual mental maps – or schema – that we carry with us into adulthood. Learning and life experiences play a major part in our psychological development in this area, but the relationships between 'causes' and 'effects' is complex. For example, witnessing violence and learning that it is somehow 'okay' to get one's way through bullying can shape a child's view of the world in a particular way. Another child, in another family, might witness violence but then live in constant fear of it happening again. Children's 'temperament' as well as the effect of all of their other experiences in life can very much shape how they interpret other events.

Social influences

These include the financial status of the family, the culture in which they live and the way that they treat each other. Families also move through life-cycle stages (Carter and McGoldrick 1989) and their success, or otherwise, at achieving these tasks will influence family members – and vice versa. Cultural and political influences as well as events on the world stage also play their part. These can obviously create fundamental limitations to the way that any family, or any child, thrives or even just survives.

Of course, there is considerable overlap and interaction between these factors. The effects can also work both ways. For instance, individuals can affect families and families can affect the individuals within them. For example, serious physical illness in one child can affect the parents' abilities to care for another child. The results are not easy to predict and will depend on a wide range of other issues. Supportive grandparents may be an enormous help in this kind of situation, whereas financial hardship, poor housing and parental ill-health will, understandably, make things more difficult.

In the rest of this chapter we will focus on some useful examples of models of child development. These are provided to set the scene for thinking about the impact of sexual abuse on development. Each 'model' concentrates on a different aspect of development but it can be useful, as described above, to try to imagine the ways that they might interact with each other.

Development across the life span

Erik Erikson (1950, 1959) established a model that mapped out development across the entire life span, or from 'cradle to grave'. He suggested that individuals move through a series of stages at more or less set periods in their lives. Each of these stages is said to revolve around a particular human issue such as 'trust' or 'independence'. The outcome of each stage steadily helps shape the individual's identity over the course of their lives. The process of growth and development is therefore seen very much as continual 'work in progress'.

Erikson also suggested that when the issues within a particular stage have not been fully dealt with, or resolved, difficulties build up and can affect the chances of successfully tackling the next stage, and so on. This idea is shared by the other theories of child development presented here, in that early difficulties are likely to create additional hurdles as the process of development carries on throughout the course of one's life.

Erikson set out a series of eight stages, and he 'mapped' these onto particular age groups. Within each stage is a central dilemma that the individual must try to deal with as well as possible, as described below.

0–1 year	Basic trust versus mistrust
2–3 years	Autonomy versus shame and doubt
4–5 years	Initiative versus guilt
6–12 years	Industry versus inferiority
13–18 years	Identity versus role confusion
19–25 years	Intimacy versus isolation
26–40 years	Generativity versus stagnation
41 years on	Ego integrity versus despair

We will return to the last three stages of this model in the next chapter when we look at the effects of childhood sexual abuse on adult development in more detail. For now, we will concentrate on the first few stages, since they tell us a great deal about the developmental 'work' that is achieved in childhood and adolescence.

1. Basic trust versus mistrust

This first stage involves the baby's development of the essential foundations of a sense of trust in others. Typically this revolves around the baby's relationship with the parents (or parent). Ideally, the parents are able to provide a safe, reliable and satisfying 'place' for their new baby within the family. The parents' behaviour towards the baby is critical to the baby's sense of security and to the development of their sense that they can affect the world in some way. For example, it is important for the baby to experience, again and again, that their parent will comfort them when they are distressed. This helps them to learn to trust. Parents who are loving and reliable and who are 'tuned in' to their baby are more likely to help their baby get through this stage well. If all goes well, these 'core' early experiences will help the baby to establish the beginnings of a firm sense of trust in themselves and in the world around them.

By comparison, parenting that is unpredictable, unresponsive and neglectful is likely to undermine the baby's trust from the outset. Furthermore, if this first step is not adequately accomplished, the baby is more likely to become the sort of child who is guarded, suspicious and defensive in relationships. So, whilst a basic sense of trust in others will tend to be carried forward positively into other relationships as the child grows up, mistrust is likely to colour relationships in a *negative* way. Correcting a basic sense of mistrust, especially when other difficulties have accumulated over time, can be an especially difficult task later in life.

2. Autonomy versus shame and doubt

Erikson's second stage occurs in the period between the ages of 2 and 3 years. This stage centres upon the child's attempts to develop a sense of independence.

Along with the rapid development of movement skills and coordination comes increasing physical mobility and freedom. If the parent is able to nurture the child's need for new experience and exploration, whilst keeping them safe and aware of danger, then the child is likely to emerge from this stage with more of a sense of independence and confidence. However, if the child's attempts at exploring the world around them have been met with harsh reprimand or overprotection, they are likely to develop a sense of shame and self-doubt instead.

Throughout further stages they are more likely than others to be inhibited and easily discouraged from trying out new things. Because of an underlying sense of incompetence, they are also less likely to embrace new opportunities to learn new skills, express their talents or develop as individuals.

3. Initiative versus guilt

The third stage occurs between 4 and 5 years of age. Once again, with a range of new and rapidly developing skills and abilities, the 'healthy' child is likely to be keen to use their initiative in order to explore the world around them. Developments in their thinking – or cognitive abilities – are also likely to mean that they are able to plan ahead and consider their actions more easily, even if they turn out to be misguided! Once again, the 'tuned in' parent is required to be attentive and available to make sure that the child is generally safe from harm.

Overall, the important issue here is for the parent to find a balance between being overbearing and intrusive on the one hand or being neglectful and disinterested on the other. Either extreme can lead to difficulties. For example, if the parent is too cautious and restrictive it may appear to the child that they were somehow 'wrong' to rely on their own initiative. This might lead them to feel that they have to suppress their natural desire to explore and experiment in order to 'fit in' and receive approval from the parent.

The child's parent has to find the balance between instilling sufficient 'wariness' in their child to prevent them from putting themselves in danger whilst also encouraging free play and experimentation. If this goes well, the child is more likely to emerge from this stage with a healthy desire to explore and a sense of their own ability to do so safely.

4. Industry versus inferiority

The fourth stage occurs roughly between 6 and 12 years of age. Perhaps another word for 'industry' in this context is a sense of competence or prowess. This stage occurs at the same time as most children are in full-time education. Since the culture demands that they achieve certain goals and learn particular skills, the child is presented with an intensive period of seeking approval and validation through learning and performing well at school.

If things do not go well, perhaps because problems arose at earlier stages, the child may experience more failure than they can cope with. Instead of a sense of competence and belief in their own abilities, they may develop a sense of inferiority. If this kind of negative self-concept stays with them over the years, then the knock-on effects are likely to be significant. For instance, the child may eventually drop out of school, believing that education has nothing to offer them. Even worse, they may also begin to feel that they have nothing to offer the world.

An attentive parent at this stage may need to recognise when to praise and when to encourage their child to try harder, or perhaps to try something else. Recognising their child's need for approval and praise at this stage may contribute an enormous amount to their child's chances of coming through this stage well.

5. Identity versus role confusion

The fifth stage occurs between 13 and 18 years of age, or from mid to late adolescence. This stage revolves around coming to terms with puberty and making the shift from childhood into the beginnings of adulthood. The adolescent has a great deal to do in terms of building an identity beyond the family. Erikson suggests that this means developing both a sexual identity and a sense of an occupational identity. Clearly both of these are major issues in terms of appreciating how any individual's life will begin to take shape once they move beyond the safety of their immediate family.

With so much going on, and so many new frontiers to be explored, it is no surprise that this can be a stormy and challenging period for the adolescent and for their family alike. During this relatively lengthy period, it is perhaps particularly important that the previous stages have been completed 'well'. It is also unsurprising that many people struggle with the many and varied challenges that come up during this period. Using Erikson's model we can begin to appreciate why this should be the case. The pressures and demands are intense, and it stands to reason that this is a time when previous difficulties are likely to show up under the strain.

It is important to appreciate that successful completion of any of these stages is not 'all or nothing' and there is room for making up ground later in life. Generally speaking, of course, it is better if the child emerges from each stage with more of the positive qualities than the negative. Clearly, the ways in which any individual manages in the adult world will depend on a great many factors including issues of temperament, circumstance and opportunity. Nevertheless, having firm foundations in each of these areas is bound to be helpful whatever challenges life holds in store.

What happens when all does not go well?

What happens when things do not go smoothly or when the child's attempts to move through these stages are undermined by damaging life events such as sexual abuse? To some degree, the answer lies in considering which 'stage' the child is in when the abuse occurs. For example, a child who experiences abuse from the age of around six is likely to have more difficulties with the third and fourth stages of development in Erikson's model. We can also predict that children abused during these periods will enter adulthood with a tendency towards 'guilt' rather than confidence and initiative. Secondly, they are more likely to emerge from childhood with a sense of 'inferiority' and 'worthlessness' rather than self-belief and confidence in their own abilities.

Using a life-span model in this way also helps to make sense of some of the indicators or signs that suggest a child is struggling as previously described. For instance, the image of a withdrawn child already burdened with a sense of guilt and stigma fits with what we might expect if a child has not passed through the third stage (Initiative versus Guilt) successfully. Similarly, the troubled teenager who 'acts-out' by angrily abandoning their studies but who is also struggling with low self-esteem becomes more understandable if we consider that their progress through the fourth stage (Industry versus Inferiority) had been made impossible because of previous abuse.

In general this model also helps us to appreciate that the earlier the abuse takes place and the more severe and prolonged the abuse has been, the more likely it will be to create difficulties that will tend to create further problems over time. In more extreme cases, in which children are abused from the earliest age, the disturbance is likely to create severe developmental problems. Overall, it is clear that abuse at any age burdens the child with less chance of coping with the particular stage of development they are going through.

Thinking and understanding – cognitive theories of development

Alongside physical growth, our mental and psychological abilities also go through enormous changes throughout childhood and adolescence. Our ability to think, remember, imagine and communicate involves various 'cognitive' abilities. These abilities complement each other, and so difficulties in one area are likely to have an effect in other areas. For instance, someone who has a poor memory can be expected to find it more difficult to communicate effectively or to make plans for the future. Likewise, someone who finds it difficult to concentrate might struggle at school.

However, 'cognitive development' also refers to the formation of ideas and beliefs we have about ourselves and about the world. Of course, these ideas can take the form of 'attitudes' and 'opinions', but they can also go much deeper in the form of 'schema' or mental maps that we carry with us into adulthood. Over time we all develop a sense of 'self' or 'identity'. As with all aspects of human development, our biology, psychology and the environment around us will all play a role in shaping how things turn out, but the beliefs we have about ourselves as people can have a dramatic effect on how we feel about ourselves *and* how we behave. We will look more closely at this when we explore how Cognitive Behavioural Therapy works by focusing explicitly on these beliefs and schema. For now, it is important to appreciate that our early experiences can influence the way we think about ourselves and others.

The beliefs we have about ourselves can be 'heard' in the way we think inside our own heads. This is sometimes referred to as 'self-talk' and describes the kind of 'conversation' we have going on in our own minds the whole time. The *kind* of self-talk each of us has will affect the way we feel and the way we behave. The quality of the self-talk we take away with us can be affected by the way we are treated as children. For example, someone who has received a lot of praise and encouragement as a child is more likely to develop positive beliefs about themselves than someone who has not. Examples might be 'I can do this' or 'I am just as good as anyone else'. By contrast, people who have been mistreated or neglected might be more likely to think 'I am no good' or 'there is something wrong with me'. Over time, it is easy to imagine how this kind of *negative thinking* can prevent you from taking part in life or from giving new things a go. Of course, that can to lead to other negative beliefs, such as 'things will never change' or 'there is no point'. In turn, this kind of bleak outlook can easily lower your mood and steadily undermine your willingness to try to see the world in a different way. The danger is that *early patterns* of negative beliefs set up a vicious circle, which just gets repeated again and again. Of course, children's abilities to think, reason and figure things out for themselves also change dramatically over time. Very young children are more likely to believe exactly what they are told. If they hear negative things being said about them all the time, or if they are treated as second rate or worthless, then they are more likely to begin to see themselves that way. Then if *bad* things keep on happening in their lives, this begins to mould the way they think about life and their future. Of course, unless things somehow change for the better, they are likely to continue to think badly of themselves as adults too.

Of course, our beliefs are always open to change. New experiences can have both negative and positive effects, and this can change our self-talk. Imagine someone who had thought things would never work out for them, but who gets a job they had really wanted. Their thoughts can begin to change as a result, such as 'If I give things a go, sometimes they work out'. This is far more optimistic than 'There is no point, nothing good ever happens to me'. Of course, the person had to be willing to put themselves forward for the job in the first place and that requires the courage to risk rejection.

Below are some theories that map out cognitive development. As always, our theories are constantly being updated and developed, but the ideas below are well known and influential. These introduce you to the idea that how we 'think' and make sense of the world changes over time. It will be clear that, at any stage, a child has different abilities to make sense of what is going on around them. Negative life events and trauma, such as sexual abuse, will be particularly difficult to handle and can mark serious shifts in self-concept and identity.

Piaget's developmental stages

Jean Piaget described how children's minds developed by taking in, or *assimilating*, new knowledge and then altering their view of the world by *accommodating* new knowledge and 'updating' their existing mental maps, or schemas. He believed that this continuous process of learning and adaptation took place across four stages, which he related to particular age groups (Piaget 1952).

The first stage, or *sensorimotor* period, is from birth to about 2 years of age. In this period the child learns through handling and interacting with objects and through repeated trial and error. The child comes to 'know' about the world through actions and through the senses. Towards the end of this period the child has acquired some internal maps of the world and has begun to 'think'.

The next stage, or *pre-operational* period, occurs between the ages of 2 and 7 years. The child's use of language becomes much more prominent and sophisticated and the child begins to develop complex internal models – or 'representations' – of the world. Their play shows much more imagination and creativity. Children in this stage become less egocentric and also begin to appreciate that other people 'think' as well. In other words they develop a 'theory of mind' and can accept that different people will see the world in different ways.

The third stage, or *concrete operational* period, takes place between the ages of 7 and 12 years. The child acquires many more 'rules' about the world around them. Their games tend to be rule-governed and they show more ability with maths and problem-solving tasks. They do this by making more use of *logic* and by thinking things through to plan their actions. They can also think around problems and consider things from a number of perspectives. This demonstrates an increasing *flexibility* in their thinking style.

The fourth stage, or *formal operational* stage, takes them into early adolescence. Children in this stage can generate ideas – or hypotheses – about problems and then come up with ways to test their ideas out. They can think things through systematically and can consider many options at the same time, rather than being too stuck on any one particular view.

Piaget's work has been greatly researched and developed over the years. However, the stages he describes provide a good starting point for reflecting on the dramatic changes that take place over a relatively short amount of time. The Information Processing Approach provides another model of cognitive development in children.

Information Processing Approach

Rather than portraying cognitive development as a series of set stages, this model describes the gradual development of a number of different 'systems' for handling information in the child's mind. For instance, 'memory' can be seen in terms of short-term *and* long-term memory systems both processing new 'information' coming in, all the time, through the senses. As these 'systems' develop with age, children become more efficient at handling information. They can gradually handle more information and they also become faster at dealing with it.

It is suggested (Noelting 1980a, 1980b) that children deal with information in distinctively different ways, as they get older. For instance, a 10-year-old can be expected to solve a problem much more quickly than a 5-year-old. The older child can also be expected to use more sophisticated methods and to *use* more information to solve the problem along the way. Older children outperform younger children because of the changes in a number of key areas. These include:

- The ability to process more information and to do so more quickly.
- The ability to focus attention and concentrate for longer.
- The development of better memory 'strategies'.
- The development of more structured knowledge about the world through learning and experience.

Taken together, these two theories cast some light on the ways in which children's minds and their ability to think about themselves and the world go through huge changes over the course of childhood and adolescence.

However, whereas Piaget's stage model and the Information Processing Approach tell us a great deal about the way children handle information and solve problems, they tell us less about how they think about themselves and others. Considering the development of particular mental maps – or schema – captures this better. In particular, the schema that we develop about ourselves as individuals are likely to have a significant bearing on the way we feel about ourselves as adults.

Schema development in childhood

We will look at the importance of schema again when we explore Cognitive Behavioural Therapy in more detail in Part IV. For now it is useful to have an overview of how the way we learn to think about ourselves as children can carry forward into adulthood. Schemas are mental patterns or blueprints about ourselves and about the world around us. They reflect the way we think about ourselves as people and how we think about our relationships.

Schemas develop in childhood and continue to be elaborated and shaped through experience and over time. Schemas can be roughly divided into 'helpful' – adaptive – schemas and 'unhelpful' – maladaptive – schemas. Schemas not only contain the ideas and beliefs we have about people and ourselves, they affect the way we feel about ourselves too. Life events can trigger schema and this can lead to particular feelings and then to particular behaviours. For instance, an adaptive schema around the issue of 'competence' could be that the person believes that they can generally look after themselves and that they can give new things a try. Again, in the example of someone looking for work, a person with an adaptive schema will think, 'I can do this, I have something to offer and I am just as good as other people'. With this in mind, they are more likely to try for the job. By contrast, someone with a negative – or maladaptive schema – may believe that they are worthless and have nothing to offer. They may also believe that 'nothing ever goes their way', and so they are much less likely to put themselves forward. The schema drives the feeling, in this case optimism or pessimism. The feeling then drives the behaviour, in this case going for the job or not.

Young (2003) suggest that maladaptive schema arise from unmet core emotional needs in childhood. He suggests five core emotional needs:

- Healthy attachments and relationships with others.
- A need for autonomy and a sense of identity.
- Liberty to express feelings and wishes.
- Spontaneity.
- A sense of realistic limits.

The child's 'temperament' (or innate character) and their early environment interact in order to satisfy or frustrate these needs. The child's family and the experiences they have as they grow up therefore play a significant role in shaping their schema, their self-concept and their outlook. When these life experiences are negative, they are more likely to give rise to maladaptive and unhelpful schema.

Young broadly identified four kinds of life experiences that can lead to maladaptive schema:

- Excessive frustration of the child's needs.
- Victimisation and trauma.
- Overprotection.
- Over-identification with others.

The first of these – *excessive frustration of the child's needs* – can lead to schema around being unlovable or unwanted. The second – *victimisation and trauma* – can lead to the expectation of further abuse and a deep sense of mistrust. The third – *overprotection* – can lead to schema around seeing oneself as entitled to 'special' treatment or as being unable to look after oneself as others are expected to. The fourth – *over-identification with others* – can lead to a poor sense of oneself as an individual or a schema around 'always being the victim'. This would be more likely to be the case if one had 'over-identified' with an aggressive or violent parent, for instance.

Of course, there are many subtle and important variations on these themes. The main aim is to highlight the many ways in which childhood experiences can become imprinted in the form of deeply held beliefs about oneself as an individual. Very often these beliefs are not challenged or even thought about consciously on a day-to-day basis. Nevertheless, they can be easily triggered by life events. For example, being unsuccessful at a job interview can have different emotional effects on people according to their particular schema.

Attachment Theory – the importance of good relationships

The central idea in Attachment Theory is that the early relationship between child and parent provides the foundations upon which trust, self-esteem and a sense of security may flourish, and hopefully persist, over the course of one's life. If this goes well, the child takes forwards a 'map' of this good relationship into adolescence and adulthood. Ideally, this helps them to form trusting relationships with other people and to generally 'engage' more fully in life. By contrast, if the opposite were true, such that early relationships were fraught with anxiety, neglect and abuse, then the child may well come to see relationships as something to be avoided. Generally, people with more 'damaging' experiences behind them are more likely to struggle to enjoy trust and intimacy in their adult relationships.

Because of its focus upon relationships, Attachment Theory is also at the heart of modern psychological therapy. Whilst methods may vary between different 'schools' of therapy, therapists all rely on an implicit appreciation of the basic importance of a sound relationship. This is reflected in the wealth of research that highlights the importance of rapport – or the working alliance – between client and therapist (Horvath and Symonds 1991; Horvath and Greenberg 1994) as an essential ingredient in successful therapy. The quality of the relationship, and the sense of trust that client and therapist are able to establish between themselves, is especially important and the gradual development of a basic sense of trust in another person can be one of the most profound achievements in a good therapeutic relationship. This makes sense, since many of us can think of friends or particular people to whom we have turned in a crisis. In many cases this may be less because of 'what' they might say or suggest and more because we knew that they would simply 'be there' when we needed them and could always be relied upon to have our best interests at heart.

In developing Attachment Theory, Bowlby (1988) began by dividing early child–parent relationships into two broad groups. He referred to these as 'secure' and 'insecure' attachments. The insecure attachment styles were then broken down into three further categories that came to be referred to as 'avoidant', 'ambivalent' and 'disorganised'.

1. Secure attachment style

Early attachment styles can be carried forward into adult life. In general, those who experienced secure attachments as children tend to have had the benefit of at least one loving parent who responded to their needs. Their parent is also likely to have held them when they needed it and let them alone when they needed time and space to explore the world around them. At school, they may have been seen as engaging and approachable. They may also have been willing to take part and to try out new things over the years.

As adults, others may see them as outgoing and as generally well-rounded people. They are also likely to have a healthy sense of self-esteem. They are likely to expect to be treated fairly by others and to feel that they deserve love and support from their partners. They are more likely to have done well at the things they have tried and to have received praise for their efforts. As a result of a combination of these generally positive experiences, they are also more likely to have the inner resources to deal with the ups and downs of everyday life. Those with the benefit of secure early attachments might also carry with them the memory of a loving parent or parental figure that has been available to them at times of need. If they suffer losses in the form of rejection, disappointment or bereavement, they are, like anyone else, likely to be distressed and to go through a process of grieving. With time, however, they are more likely to 'bounce back' and to feel willing and able to engage in life once again, knowing that life always entails change and loss, but that the reward is generally worth any pain.

The parents of securely attached children tend to be 'tuned in' to their children and are generally responsive to their needs. This kind of parent successfully walks the line between being sufficiently available to their child without becoming overly intrusive or overprotective. They are also reliable 'enough' to create, in the child's mind, a sense that they are safe and that someone will come to help them if they are upset or in trouble. Overall, their attention towards their child is active and responsive. More often than not, it is the 'quality' of the time they spend with their children that counts far more than the 'quantity'.

2. Insecure-avoidant attachment style

At school, children who have experienced insecure-avoidant attachments may be withdrawn, standoffish or even hostile towards other children. These can be understood as the outward signs of their efforts to avoid dependency and to distance themselves from others in order to feel less anxious. At times, their frustration may erupt in angry outbursts. This outward hostility can mask a deep vulnerability and a fear of 'need', which is quickly hidden away for fear of provoking further rejection. In general, they are difficult to get close to and they may continue to have difficulties feeling that they can trust anyone for long.

As adults, people with this kind of background might be so distrustful of others and so convinced of other people's unreliability that they keep themselves emotionally distant. They may be always prepared to 'move on' and never feel that they have really put down their roots. Of course, behind the scenes, they may be desperate to find someone whom they can really trust, but their suspicion and doubt are likely to continue to be major hurdles for them. In attempting to 'get the better' of their anxieties they may come across as cold and distant. However, people in this group can also tend to be over-controlling and domineering in their relationships. This might be an attempt to make sure that others cannot get away and cannot become unreliable, as their own parents had been. The issue of distrust is central either way.

The parents of children in this group tend to have been unresponsive to their child's needs. For any number of reasons, they may have struggled to offer enough physical contact, warmth and love to their children. This may have meant that they did not respond to their baby's distress or else reacted with anger and frustration. They may have also chosen to ignore or reject their children's attempts at contact and communication as time went on. Generally speaking, there will have been less interaction between parent and child. Furthermore, time spent together might have been more 'functional' or task-oriented rather than based around enjoyment or shared experience. For whatever reason, the parents do not appear to have 'tuned in' to their children.

3. Insecure-ambivalent attachment style

Children who have developed an insecure-ambivalent attachment style will tend to shift between clinging to the parent on one hand and angrily rejecting them on the other. Others can then perceive them as being unpredictable and 'difficult'. In friendships, they are likely to 'blow hot and cold' as they anxiously shift between different strategies for managing close relationships. Emotionally, they are likely to be volatile and difficult to comfort. They may feel both crushed *and* enraged when they experience rejection by their friends or peers. They can be very sensitive to the early signs that they are being pushed away and can misinterpret the intentions of others.

As adults, people with this kind of history are likely to be more volatile and impulsive in relationships. Because they fear that other people are unpredictable, they may shift unpredictably between being clingy and overbearing or else being moody and withdrawn. In trying to stay 'one step ahead' of the abandonment they dread, they may be constantly trying to second-guess their partner and trying to finally get 'control' over the person upon whom they now depend.

The parents of children in this group tend to have been inconsistent in responding to their child's needs. This may have left the child believing that 'sometimes' their parent was available, whilst at others they were not; but with no reliable pattern for them to hang on to. This may have led them to believe that their parents could not be relied upon to be there for them when needed. The child may then have tried to 'cling' to the parent on some occasions, whilst angrily protesting and pushing them away on others. Once this pattern has been established the inconsistency on the part of parent *and* child is likely to continue to make life difficult for both of them.

4. Insecure-disorganised attachment style

Less common are those children who could be described as having developed an insecure-disorganised attachment style. This pattern is associated with more severe neglect and with physical and sexual abuse. Children in this category will tend to be extremely watchful of others. Their caution and suspicion may lead to a noticeable lack of spontaneity. For example, their 'play' might well be particularly inhibited and restricted. They are likely to find it very difficult to engage with others because of their underlying fear.

As adults, people with this kind of background may find the process of forming lasting relationships extremely difficult. They may be highly unpredictable and impulsive and deeply wounded by rejection or by any signs of imminent abandonment. They may be very unsure as to what to expect from a partner and are likely to be highly vulnerable to exploitation and domination by others.

The parents of children in this group tend to have been physically and emotionally abusive and to have exposed their children to a significant degree of chaos, neglect and maltreatment. Of course, this may have been partly as a result of their own severe psychological or emotional difficulties as adults. Hence, this type of attachment pattern is observed more often in the children of parents with marked emotional difficulties of one kind or another.

Do attachment styles persist over time?

Researchers such as Mary Ainsworth and colleagues (1978) provided the clinical findings behind Bowlby's early works on Attachment Theory. In her work as a developmental psychologist, Ainsworth devised a test of parenting style, known as the Strange Situation. In this test both parent and child (typically at the age of 1 or 2 years) were invited into a playroom along with a member of the research team. A team of researchers recorded events in the room. After having a few minutes to settle in, the parent was asked to leave the room, leaving the child with the experimenter. After three minutes the parent returned and there was a brief period of reunion between parent and child. Shortly afterwards, both parent and researcher left the room, this time leaving the child on their own. After a further three minutes the parent returned for a second reunion. The interaction between parent and child was then analysed by observers, paying particular attention to the child's behaviour at each point of separation and reunion.

The team identified the four basic patterns of child behaviour, as described by Bowlby in his development of Attachment Theory. For instance, children whom the team described as securely attached were usually upset by the separation. When the parent returned they would greet and acknowledge them in some way. However, having sought and received comfort, they would tend to settle quickly and then return to playing contentedly as before.

By contrast, children in the insecure-avoidant group tended to show few outward signs of distress at the separation. Curiously, they would also appear to ignore the parent upon their return. Upon reunion, these children also tended to remain watchful of their parent and rather inhibited in their style of play. This apparent indifference tended to be even more marked upon the second reunion, when it might be expected that the upset of repeated and unpredictable separations would have been at its height.

Children whom the team placed in the insecure-ambivalent category tended to be highly distressed by the separation. They also tended to be more difficult to settle upon the parent's return. When they did seek contact with the parent they reacted aggressively or else turned away, resisting attempts by the parent to offer comfort. In general these children also tended to be rather inhibited in their play and shifted between clinging to the parent or else angrily pushing them away.

The fourth group of children, whom the team placed in the insecure-disorganised category, tended to show more extreme behaviours upon separation. They appeared extremely confused and disorientated, and generally showed more alarming and unusual behaviours such as 'freezing', as if they really did not know how to react.

As with other areas of research, our knowledge is always developing, but it seems that the prevalence of these patterns is more or less stable over time. Generally speaking, research suggests that around 65 per cent of children can be categorised as secure, 20 per cent as insecure-avoidant, 10–15 per cent as insecure-ambivalent with a variable proportion of the remainder as insecure-disorganised (van Ijzendoorn and Kroonenburg 1988), although there are some variations between different cultures. However, the most consistent predictor of child behaviour seems to be the degree of 'disturbance' within the family.

Importantly, the ratio of these percentages is different when assessing families in which there has been a history of physical and/or sexual abuse. Generally speaking, in families where abuse has occurred, only 10 per cent of the children can be categorised as secure, 30 per cent are usually found to be insecure-disorganised with the remainder falling into the insecure-avoidant or insecure-ambivalent groups (Belsky and Nezworski 1988).

Once the child has an internal working model of relationships, this can set the scene for how they experience and behave within their close relationships in the future. Further research has demonstrated that early attachment styles can continue unchanged over time. However, they can change in response to both positive and negative life events within the family (Vaughan *et al.* 1979). Other studies have found that early attachment styles can sometimes continue for many years (Main and Cassidy 1988; Grossman and Grossman 1991; Waters *et al.* 2000). There is also some evidence to suggest that attachment styles can carry over from one generation to the next, presumably due to the effect this can have on one's own parenting style (van Ijzendoorn 1995).

Of course, it is important to remember that these patterns are not 'set in stone' and that positive life events and relationships can help to balance out negative early experiences. The optimism in this idea provides one of the cornerstones of modern psychological therapy. For instance, if a child has learnt that the world is full of frightening, unpredictable and unreliable people, and if life has continued to replay this message to them as an adult, then the safe and reliable environment of therapy may be one place where some of their basic assumptions can be looked at again. One aim of psychological therapy is to allow the person to steadily chip away at their long-held assumptions about themselves and other people and to try out new ideas. This process is a central part of the work of successful therapy.

7 What happens if things go wrong?

All of the models described earlier in Part II emphasise the importance of early experiences and the parent–child relationship in
providing the foundations for an individual's future development.
Childhood sexual abuse has immediate and long-term effects on this
process. In this chapter we will look at these effects in turn.

There is now a wealth of clinical and research evidence identifying
the negative effects of childhood sexual abuse across the full range
of functioning (Finkelhor and Browne 1986b; Kendall-Tackett *et al.*
1993; Fergusson and Mullen 1999). In particular, the immediate
developmental consequences of childhood sexual abuse can affect the
following:

* emotional health
* behaviour
* cognitive functioning and achievement
* physical health
* relationships and social behaviour.

Emotional health

The initial effects of sexual abuse upon a child's emotional well-being
can be seen in wide-ranging changes in their demeanour. Examples
are fearfulness, anxiety and withdrawal from others. Certain children
may develop tics or anxiety-based habits, such as excessive nail-biting
or hair-pulling. There can be changes in the child's eating and sleeping
habits, especially if their anxiety carries on for an appreciable amount
of time. Specific fears and phobias might also develop. It may appear
that these have come 'out of the blue', but they may also relate to
particular aspects of the abuse. For example, being left with particular
people or being in certain rooms may remind the child of times when

awful things happened to them. The symptoms of anxiety such as nightmares, flashbacks and dissociation (feeling 'spaced out') may be so intense as to suggest the presence of Post-Traumatic Stress Disorder (PTSD).

Children who have been abused may show signs of depression, such as flattened mood, lack of energy and a lack of spontaneity. In older children, depression may also reflect the guilt and shame they are feeling as well as their hopelessness, especially if the abuse is still going on. At its worst, depression can lead to suicidal thoughts and acts of self-harm.

Some children react by becoming generally more emotionally unpredictable and extreme in their reactions around other people. This might mean, for example, that their temper flares up more quickly and that they are more aggressive with other children. In school, a sexually abused child may also begin to behave in a noticeably more disruptive and antisocial way with others.

Long-term effects might include the worsening of any of the above symptoms, along with the development of other conditions related to chronic emotional distress. For instance, suffering from anxiety over a long period of time is likely to lead to exhaustion and a range of physical problems. It can also increase the risk of developing secondary symptoms such as depression. Adults who have suffered sexual abuse as children frequently report severe depressive conditions. Depression, in turn, can increase the risk of self-harm, and lead to suicidal thoughts and behaviour. Chronic low mood also increases the likelihood of substance misuse. Additional symptoms such as dissociation can also continue into the long term. Dissociative symptoms are also often linked to a broad range of other symptoms, including nightmares, flashbacks, excessive anger and low self-esteem – all of which are associated with PTSD. The risk is that one difficulty can lead to another, so that problems accumulate.

Behaviour

Children who have been sexually abused may express their distress through their behaviour. If this is the case, then it may be particularly noticeable to others when a child's behaviour changes unexpectedly. This is easier to spot in the absence of any other obvious causes, such as a change of school or some other disruption in the child's routine. Whilst some abused children tend to 'shut down' and withdraw at school, others may appear to become more hyperactive. As a result, they find it difficult to concentrate or to behave well in class. They may attempt to distract others or seek attention in disruptive ways that are difficult for others to ignore. More highly visible signs of distress include truancy from school or running away from home.

Case example – Anna

Like many children Anna appeared to struggle with the move from junior school to secondary school. This big transition also coincided with traumatic and abusive events at home. Although these were short-lived, they left Anna reeling and overwhelmed. Her sense of certainty and security had been turned upside down and the last thing she needed was another big change to deal with. In order to protect herself, she became withdrawn and she tended to isolate herself from others. Because Anna's new teachers were unaware of quite how much she had changed in such a short space of time, they assumed this was just the way she was.

Anna had one or two friends, but found mixing with others difficult and she did not feel comfortable around the older children. The rough and tumble of the playground upset her and she found participating in class activities awkward and embarrassing.

In this example, Anna turned inward and became more inhibited and withdrawn over time. Other children who have been abused can become more aggressive and begin to bully and intimidate others, especially children whom they see as weaker than themselves. In acting-out or displaying their feelings in this way, they may find a temporary outlet for some of the bad feelings they are experiencing.

At the other end of the scale, another extreme behaviour change is sometimes referred to as 'total refusal syndrome'. In this scenario the child withdraws to their room and refuses to participate in any way at all.

Some children may also show a preoccupation with sexual talk, sexual play and masturbation that seems to be in advance of their years. They might begin to encourage other children into sexual acts that mimic the things that have been done to them. The problem of children's abuse of each other is relatively under-researched. However, it is being increasingly recognised as an area of childhood sexual abuse that requires further investigation (Farmer and Pollock 2005; Sperry and Gilbert 2005).

Long-term effects of the kinds of behavioural disturbances outlined above include a gradual worsening of challenging and disruptive behaviour. For instance, a child or adolescent might eventually earn something of a 'reputation' for their delinquency and aggression. Such an 'identity' might be difficult to shake off. Long-term patterns of disruptive behaviour are also likely to have a serious impact upon a child's achievement in school. The risk is that this leads to chronic self-esteem difficulties and a gradual narrowing of opportunities in their adult life.

Cognitive functioning and achievement

A child's ability to think, learn and concentrate can also be affected by sexual abuse. The effects can sometimes be seen in the failure of a child to thrive at school and in a generally poor attainment in the absence of any other clear underlying causes or conditions that might be expected to affect learning. As with the other areas discussed so far, one might expect to see a marked decline in a child's performance at school in the wake of recent abuse or during a period of ongoing abuse. For example, the child may appear distracted at school or may appear to find it difficult to concentrate. Their attention span is especially likely to suffer if they are preoccupied with trying to make sense of an experience that frightened and unsettled them. For older children, signs such as a noticeable deterioration in achievement might suggest that they are performing below their potential for no obvious reason.

Over time a developmental delay can also build up. If this happens, a child could fall further and further behind, possibly earning a reputation for being disinterested and disruptive and steadily drifting away from school. If this goes on for any appreciable amount of time the child may feel that there is no point in trying to catch up. They may assume that they are not *able* to do the work and they might disengage from learning altogether. As more and more of the building blocks of a good education are missed, each subsequent hurdle presents more of a challenge. Of course, this is only likely to increase the risk of early withdrawal from school, leading to more difficulties when it comes to establishing a place in the world of work. This kind of vicious circle is easy to imagine and is one in which the person's self-esteem and confidence are both likely to remain at rock bottom.

Physical health

Children's bodies are not designed for sex. It is obvious that particular sexual acts with a child, especially those involving penetration of any kind, are likely to lead to wounding and physical injuries. Some possible signs of childhood sexual abuse are rectal or genital bleeding, soreness and itching. However, it must be remembered that there may be other causes for these symptoms besides sexual abuse. Other possible signs include repeated genito-urinary infections and there may also be evidence of internal scarring.

Other physical symptoms might include abdominal pains, pain upon urination and defecation and occasional difficulties with standing or moving. If physical force and restraint were used during the sexual abuse then there may be visible marks caused by the accompanying physical abuse. These might include bruising, perhaps in the form of grip marks as well as bites, cuts, tears and scalds. There may also be signs of partial suffocation, which may have been used to silence the child or terrify them into submission.

Understandably, the long-term physical effects of childhood sexual abuse are as many and varied as the initial symptoms. Depending upon the child's stage of physical development and the degree of injury caused, it is easy to imagine that a significant proportion of adults who were sexually abused as children still bear the physical signs in some way. This might be reflected in terms of recurrent pain, scarring or chronic physical conditions that are directly related to the original trauma. Since physical abuse and sexual abuse are strongly associated with each other, the risk of one is automatically heightened in the presence of the other.

Apart from the more obvious signs of physical damage, wounding and infection outlined above, there are many other physical symptoms that have been associated with the after-effects of sexual abuse in childhood. These symptoms can often be seen as a secondary result of the emotional difficulties triggered by the abuse and trauma. They are often referred to as psychosomatic symptoms. This term is often misunderstood so as to suggest that the symptoms are somehow not real or are a figment of the person's imagination. This is not the intended meaning at all. Psychosomatic symptoms are usually the result of prolonged and acute emotional distress. For instance, chronic anxiety can lead to insomnia and marked changes in appetite that can persist for long periods of time. The same can apply in some cases of frequent headaches, stomach-aches and constipation. Sometimes these symptoms do not respond to straightforward treatments and show no obvious physical cause. More severe symptoms include persistent enuresis (wetting) and encopresis (soiling) beyond the age that one would expect the child to have developed control over them.

Relationships and social behaviour

As above, children who have been abused may react in a variety of ways. Some may become rather withdrawn and reclusive. These children are likely to be seen as unlikable and are at further risk of being ostracised and rejected by others. Other children who have been sexually abused may turn their feelings outwards and become quite cruel towards others around them. Both groups are unlikely to form good relationships with peers or teachers and they may well be seen as difficult and immature. For all of these troubled children, friendships are likely to be short-lived and their relationships are likely to be characterised by conflict and uncertainty.

If shame and guilt are marked features of the child's response to the abuse, then this is something else that is likely to lead them to isolate themselves and perhaps to angrily push others away. Once again, it may be the relatively *sudden* nature of changes in a child's behaviour along these lines that is most noticeable to others.

As children move through adolescence and into early adulthood, additional difficulties can emerge. These can be understood as some of the more long-term effects of the original abuse. For example, some people who have been abused react to the trauma by behaving in a promiscuous or sexually provocative way in later life. The reasons for this are many and varied, and may include the search for attention and love through sex; perhaps because the person feels that this is all they have to offer. Promiscuity and risky sexual behaviour can also be ways of temporarily releasing some of the tension and distress associated with the original trauma. Some people cope with sexual trauma by coming to believe that they 'do not matter' and that their bodies 'do not matter' either. For someone with this kind of negative self-image, the shift into prostitution or some other form of degradation might be a real risk.

For others, promiscuity and sexually provocative behaviour can be seen as an attempt at gaining some kind of control, or 'mastery', over the original abuse. It is as if the person is saying to themselves 'these things upset me when I was a child but now I am in charge and I am deciding when and how these things take place'. From another perspective, it may seem to others that they are actually treating themselves with very little self-respect. An extreme example may be someone who shifts into committing abusive acts themselves, telling themselves that since these things were done to them, it is now their 'turn'. The heavy burden of responsibility not to repeat the abuse in any way is obviously a very serious issue and is central to a consideration of the long-term effects of childhood abuse. We will return to this issue again in Part III, when we consider the effects upon adults in more depth.

Case example – Sarah

Sarah seemed fine at school. As she went into adolescence she began dating and was more sexually advanced and adventurous than most of her friends. She tended to attract older boys who were also sexually active, but the relationships did not seem to last long. Boys often lost interest in her quite quickly and moved on.

Curiously, if anyone treated her well and was more interested in her as a person, Sarah pushed them away. She did not understand why she did this, but it became something of a pattern.

When she felt 'up', Sarah could be the life and soul of the party and she seemed to have a lot of friends. If a boyfriend rejected her, Sarah would shrug it off as if nothing had happened. Others sometimes perceived her as quite cold as a result. In any case, because of her outgoing personality she soon had another boyfriend. However, behind her façade Sarah began to feel lonely and worthless. She could not figure out why her friends could keep their boyfriends whereas she could not.

Of course, in terms of sexuality and sexual relationships, others may take a completely different path than in this case example. They might enter adolescence and adulthood burdened with the same feelings of shame and confusion, but attempt to cope with it through inhibition. For these people sexual relationships continue to be a source of awkwardness, embarrassment and fear. Obviously the impact upon one's quality of life and general sense of well-being is likely to be considerable. However, like many of the issues outlined above, these issues can be a focus of therapeutic work at a later stage.

An important note of caution

It is very important to appreciate that these signs and symptoms are not *proof* in and of themselves that a child either is being, or has been, sexually abused. However, because they signal *distress*, they obviously warrant attention in terms of flagging up the possibility that something is wrong, whatever the cause turns out to be.

There are, of course, many reasons why a child might suddenly appear withdrawn and distant. There might be current conflict in their parents' relationship or the child may simply be concerned about an event in their lives that is entirely appropriate for their age and development, such as an argument with a close friend. Clearly, what is important is for those people in the child's life at the time to at least be aware of the danger signs and to have the courage and concern to ask the right questions and to express their concern. At the very least, this shows children that adults do notice what is happening and can pick up on their signals.

8 Risk factors and a useful summary

What are the risk factors for childhood sexual abuse?

With our knowledge of the essentials of healthy development in mind, it might be useful to take another look at the types of situations in which abuse appears to occur more frequently. From this perspective it should become clear that it is by no means just 'bad luck' that these things continue to happen in certain situations. More often, a combination of risk factors can be identified.

Before we proceed, it is important to remember that because disclosure rates have been low and a vast amount of the abuse that takes place remains hidden, a precise knowledge of the risk factors also remains elusive. The list below has been put together by looking at the circumstances in the lives of children where a history of abuse has been confirmed. What is clear from the available evidence is that whilst childhood sexual abuse occurs across virtually all kinds of social and family circumstances, there are particular factors that have been linked to an increased risk of abuse occurring in any situation. These include:

Gender

Girls, overall, may be more than twice as likely as boys to experience childhood sexual abuse.

Age

Overall, the period of greatest risk appears to be between the ages of 4 and 12 years. Girls are at even greater risk between the ages of 10 and 12 years.

Social isolation

Having few friends and being generally isolated from others appear to be linked to childhood sexual abuse.

Family relationships

The absence of one or both parents during childhood has been linked to higher rates of sexual abuse. Ongoing parental conflict and poor child–parent relationships – particularly between mother and child – have also been linked to greater levels of sexual abuse. The presence of stepfathers has also been linked to an increased risk of the occurrence of sexual abuse within the family.

Other difficulties

The absence of one's biological parents can be a risk factor. Also, parental disability, illness, psychiatric history and/or drug addiction have all been linked to higher rates of sexual abuse. This is probably because these factors can sometimes make it difficult to provide adequate parental supervision.

Of course, these are generalisations and the presence of one, or more, of these risk factors does not automatically mean that abuse will occur and, of course, every situation is different in some way. However, if we bear in mind what we have learnt about the kinds of environment children need in order to develop healthily, then it is clear that situations in which there are multiple problems are also more likely to be situations in which neglect and lack of attention to childcare are more commonplace.

Why do certain situations present more risk of abuse?

There are many ways to understand this. For example, a child who has grown up in an atmosphere of conflict and neglect and the absence of, let's say, their biological father may well crave attention from adults. If they have not been fortunate enough to experience clear relationship boundaries from a loving parent, then they may not know what to expect from others. If an adult comes into their lives and shows them the attention that has been missing, then they are likely to find it difficult to resist. If this attention is then gradually combined with acts of an increasingly sexual nature then, step-by-step, the child can end up feeling trapped and obligated. This is referred to as 'grooming'. It is the process by which the adult abuser slowly but surely wins the trust and affection of the child and then gradually transforms what appears to be a friendly, or even 'apparently' loving, relationship into a sexually abusive one. The child may then feel to blame, since they may believe that they *agreed* to take part in some way. If they accepted the treats and the attention, they may feel guilty and trapped and as if they are as much to blame as the adult. If they have become accustomed to the attention and if some of the sexual acts were apparently physically 'enjoyable' (despite their being unable to make sense of them emotionally), then they may feel completely ensnared in the situation. Even worse, they may assume that because they have 'taken part', they are obviously 'bad' or 'dirty' in some way. If the shame is such that they cannot speak out, then the situation is all the more distressing.

It is important to take a moment to link this back to the information presented earlier in Part II on the initial effects of sexual abuse. A child caught in this situation is likely to experience any number of the symptoms listed, including withdrawal, anxiety and depression. Meanwhile any existing sense of self-worth and healthy self-image is likely to be severely undermined in the process.

Case example – Sarah

The man who abused Sarah did not physically threaten her. Nor did he ever physically hurt her. He did not need to use physical force because he created a situation in which he could use emotional force to more effect. Sarah had already suffered upheaval in her life. By talking to her and her mother, he realised that this was something Sarah wanted to avoid and this became a lever for him to use against her. By helping Sarah's mum, he became part of the fabric of their lives. By giving Sarah 'secret' gifts and extra pocket money, he began to buy her compliance and to create a split in the relationship, one where Sarah would be rewarded for keeping secrets from her mum.

As he began to change their relationship into a sexual one, the abuser was always ready to confront Sarah with the consequence of her speaking out. He said he would stop helping her mum and that they would then have to move. He also said that he would tell her mum that she was 'naughty' and that she had been stealing from him. Sarah panicked and the longer she waited, the more difficult it seemed to speak out. She was trapped between her mum, the abuser and her own wish to hang on to her new home and friends. Because he knew this, the abuser would always believe he had the upper hand.

If we look at this all-too-familiar scenario through the lens provided by the models of child development discussed above, then we can see, once again, that the sexual abuse of children is an exploitation of their bodies, their minds and their feelings. The after-effects of this are highly likely to change the course of their lives. Sarah was caught in a very confusing situation. She was worried about being blamed and understandably frightened of the consequences of saying 'no'. It is unsurprising that she felt powerless to speak out under all of this pressure. For Sarah, as for many people, it may have seemed that there was no-one 'safe' to talk to about what was happening to her, even if she could have found the words to begin to explain. As above, social isolation and being cut off from people one can trust is an added risk factor for many children.

Putting it together

So far in Part II we have covered a lot of ground. We have looked in detail at child development. This has included taking a 'life-span' view as well as looking more specifically at intellectual development and the importance of relationships in childhood. We then looked at some of the signs and symptoms that tell us that the child is in distress. We also considered how sexual abuse can affect development in many different ways, as well as about some of the risk factors associated with increased levels of abuse. It is a lot to take in. For that reason I want to return to the model introduced to you briefly in Part I. It is called the Traumagenic Dynamics model and was developed by David Finkelhor and Angela Browne (Finkelhor and Browne 1986a). Because it is so brief, it is a great way of pulling together much of what we have just covered.

Finkelhor and Browne's Traumagenic Dynamics

Once again, this model highlights four basic aspects of the trauma and disturbance that can result from childhood sexual abuse. These are:

- sexual traumatisation
- betrayal
- stigmatisation
- powerlessness.

Next, we will consider each heading in turn, but in more detail than before. Read through each one in turn and stop at the end of each section to reflect on what you have just read. If you think that it applies to you, take a few minutes to reflect and then maybe write your thoughts down. How did this affect you as a child, and how does it affect you now? Which seems to be most important area for you, or do you recognise that more than one of the areas continues to be difficult for you? Taking the time to think about this now will help you when, in Part IV, I ask you to begin thinking about how you would want therapy to help you. By having a focus early on, you will be giving yourself a head start.

Sexual traumatisation

Sexual traumatisation occurs because the child's body and mind are unable to cope with the experience of sex. Physically they are not equipped to cope with sex, and because they are unable to understand what it means they cannot cope with the emotional consequences either. For example, a child who receives extra attention or treats in return for sexual acts may completely confuse sex with love. They may begin to believe that they always have to *earn* love in this way or that they are being bad if they do not go along with what others want from them. Children do not understand boundaries in relationships, they have to be shown them and this is the responsibility of the adults in their lives. The adult who crosses any sexual boundary with a child has broken the trust that should exist between a child and an adult and shattered a most important boundary. This leaves the child with little chance to work out where the boundaries really are in their relationships.

This intense confusion is likely to have dramatic effects in adult life when it comes to dealing with adult relationships. The person who was sexually abused as a child may feel that they still have to earn love through taking part in sexual relationships that they do not enjoy. They may feel that they are not allowed to say 'no' or that their partner somehow owns the rights to their body because they provide for them in other ways. They may also struggle to tell the difference between intimacy and exploitation. Of course, they may go to the other extreme and find any sexual contact disturbing and uncomfortable because it reminds them of the original abuse. Either way, the possibility of establishing a healthy and enjoyable sex life, based upon loving respect for one another, becomes more difficult to achieve.

Betrayal

This is an extremely powerful word. Betrayal is at the very centre of childhood sexual abuse. As above, children are simply not equipped to cope with the overwhelming emotional impact of sexual abuse. We have already seen how important it is that children can really trust the people around them to keep them safe if they are to develop healthily. If the fundamental belief that your parent will not harm or exploit you is shattered, then the sense of betrayal that results can cause a very deep emotional wound.

In order to cope with such an overwhelming challenge to their beliefs about the people they depend on, children may resort to rationalising their feelings away. For instance, they may force themselves to believe that it is somehow okay for these things to happen to them or that they are bad and somehow deserve to be treated this way. Similarly, they might convince themselves that they are special in some way or that these awful things are not really happening to them at all. In short, children may try to believe *anything* rather than accept the awful truth of what is happening to them. If they were to accept that they really were that unsafe, especially if the abuse happened at home, then the anxiety might be completely overwhelming. In an attempt to make sense of something that they are not equipped to understand, children sometimes learn to bend the truth in their own minds so as to protect themselves from the reality of what is happening. The cost of this distortion of reality can be enormous. At worst it can lead people to cling to delusional beliefs about themselves and the world, which can be very difficult to challenge.

Stigmatisation

Stigmatisation occurs because the experience of sexual abuse can leave children feeling different to others in a very negative way. Children who have been sexually abused often feel 'dirty' or as if they are 'damaged goods' in one way or another. If this becomes part and parcel of the child's identity, then they are very likely to suffer from low self-esteem and to feel worthless. They may feel that they deserve nothing better than to be treated badly and find themselves caught up in abusive relationships again and again. They may feel unable to assert themselves and unable to see that they may deserve more from life. Meanwhile they may be left wondering why they always seem to attract the wrong kind of partners.

Stigma also brings a heavy burden of shame. This can leave people feeling that others also see them in a negative and disapproving light. It may be that one reason why disclosure rates are so low is that children feel so ashamed and so worried about bringing shame upon the family that they keep the secret to themselves. Perhaps they hope that one day the sense of shame will dissolve away. Shame can prevent people from coming forward to disclose what has happened and it can also prevent them from coming into therapy. Of course, working through the burden of shame that results from childhood sexual abuse can be a very important aspect of any therapeutic work.

Powerlessness

A sense of powerlessness inevitably follows from the exploitation of one person's control over another. This is a basic feature of abuse, sexual or otherwise. Children are abused by people in a position of power over them, including other children. More typically it is a parent, guardian or authority figure of some kind. Threats, force and other forms of coercion are often used, all of which represent a misuse of power. If a child is intimidated and then coerced into a sexual act, then their powerlessness has been deliberately exploited.

Clearly, this kind of experience can leave children feeling trapped, defenceless and increasingly hopeless. The roots of depression are clearly visible in this kind of experience. In addition, once the person is free from the abusive situation, a sense of outrage and fury can linger for many years to come. Outbursts of aggression, often at the 'wrong' target, can be especially upsetting for everyone involved. If this turns out to be the result of the rage that had to be held in as a child, then it may well continue to resurface time and again. This is especially likely to happen when, as an adult, the person feels betrayed or exploited in some way. However, the intense feelings that get stirred up may seem completely out of proportion with the current situation. Once again, reflecting upon the possible connection between these feelings and the anger that had to be hidden away in childhood can be another step towards undoing the influence of the past on the present.

This model is especially useful alongside the other models of child development described above, because it focuses very clearly on why sexual abuse in childhood is so damaging. To feel traumatised, betrayed, stigmatised and powerless is a potentially overwhelming combination.

Review and exercise

In Part II we looked at some models of child development. These models emphasised the role of sound early relationships in shaping an individual's development. Putting these ideas together allowed us to look more closely at the initial and long-term effects of sexual abuse on child development.

At this stage, and with the benefit of an overview of healthy development, it is hopefully easier to see how problems might well carry over into adulthood after abuse in childhood. Research so far has suggested that early intervention, in the form of psychological therapy and support, can have beneficial effects (Finkelhor and Berliner 1995; Deblinger et al. 2006). However, the number of children who access this is a tiny minority compared to the numbers who experience abuse. This may well be because there is a shortfall in the provision of services. It may also be the case, especially when there are complicated family circumstances, that the chances of anyone speaking out at the time are still relatively slim.

By contrast, it is probably more likely that a sexually abused child will come to the attention of the educational authorities or health services for all the 'wrong' reasons, such as their 'bad' behaviour or perhaps their lack of achievement at school. It is often similar in the case of adults, who come to psychiatric services with alcohol problems or a history of self-harm. Once again, the underlying causes of these problems are often easy to miss in the midst of a psychiatric or medical crisis.

As has been suggested throughout this book, it may be worth spending some time at this point reflecting upon what you have taken from Part II before moving on.

Perhaps you recognised something of your own childhood here. For instance, in the details on Attachment Theory you may have identified with one of the groups more than others. This may have brought particular aspects of your childhood back into your thoughts. If this is the case, then try to stay with what you are feeling and note down some key words that come to mind. If you decided to begin a journal or a diary of your thoughts and feelings, then you might try going into more detail at this stage. For instance, do you recognise some of the patterns of relationships described above and have they stayed with you as an adult? Looking back, do you sometimes cling anxiously to partners and then angrily push them away, making it impossible for either of you to feel settled or secure? Are you someone who can be relaxed in relationships or does life feel so full of anxiety and threat that you do not ever feel secure enough to do so? Have these patterns influenced how you react to other people in your adult life as well as your own children, if you have them?

Spotting these patterns and recognising them is an essential first step in making changes. Once you know what is wrong, it is much easier to decide what to do next in order to go about putting things right.

In Part III we will look in more detail at the types of difficulties adults may experience as a result of a history of childhood sexual abuse.

Part III

Childhood sexual abuse and adulthood

9 Introduction

From past to present

In Part III we will pay much more attention to the kinds of problems that affect adults. In particular, we will look more closely at the range of symptoms and conditions that have been linked to childhood sexual abuse. Once again, it is very important to appreciate that the presence of any of these conditions does not automatically *prove* that the sufferer has been sexually abused. There are many other possible causes for the conditions described here. If sexual abuse has been a part of your history, then it may well have left you with some ongoing problems. However, there may be many other reasons for the difficulties you are experiencing and sexual abuse may be only one aspect of this. For this reason, it is always recommended that you think these things through carefully. Then talk it through with your GP or a mental health professional, who will be able to help you by asking the right questions.

We will begin by continuing our exploration of the life plan development model whilst looking at the tasks and challenges of adult development that take us through to old age. Many of the common symptoms and conditions that have been linked with childhood sexual abuse will be described. The various diagnoses will be explained in more detail and the jargon will be broken down so that you can talk to professionals about these things with more confidence. After that we will focus on Post-Traumatic Stress Disorder (PTSD). This condition has been strongly linked to childhood sexual abuse and it is important to have good understanding of it. If it applies directly to you, then being familiar with the ideas behind it will put you in a better position to engage with therapy. Finally, we will move on to consider personality disorders. Once again, particular diagnoses such as Borderline Personality Disorder have been strongly linked with

82   *Moving on after childhood sexual abuse*

childhood sexual abuse. A diagnosis of Personality Disorder can be frightening and confusing. By breaking the diagnosis down, it will become less daunting and the separate aspects can be thought about in turn. As a result, it becomes less of a 'label' and more a way of describing a particular pattern of deep-seated difficulties. Then there will be more chance of it becoming a starting point for decision-making about how to make changes.

Echoes of the past

As described in Part II, the effects of childhood sexual abuse can be very serious and wide-ranging. Firstly, there are the initial effects seen in children and adolescents. These signs are more likely to be noticeable whilst the abuse is happening or shortly after it has stopped. Then there are the long-term effects, which can continue into late adolescence and adulthood. Of course, some of these later difficulties are similar to the earlier problems, such as symptoms of anxiety and depression. However, we also know that particular problems can build up over time. In Part III we will explore these long-term difficulties in more detail.

In Part II we saw that the difficulties acquired in childhood could affect many different aspects of an individual's 'functioning'. The effects could be seen in terms of negative patterns of thoughts, feelings, behaviour and relationships. Of course, all of these areas are central to your health, happiness and well-being as an adult too. The long-term effects of childhood sexual abuse can continue to influence you across these key areas.

Just as in childhood, problems can also become intertwined. This means that difficulties in one area can increase the likelihood of problems in another.

Case example – Mark

Mark left school early. He was relieved to get away from home, but he did not have much of a plan as to where to go next. He felt he had to sacrifice his education for a sense of freedom. Behind his outgoing demeanour, Mark was actually quite anxious and insecure. He often tried to boost his confidence by drinking and using cannabis. These deadened his anxiety for a while, but also created other problems for him along the way. For instance, Mark sometimes struggled to cope at work after numerous late nights. This caused conflicts at work and

Mark did not handle the criticism well. He also felt tired all the time and it did not take much for him to feel like giving up.

Behind the scenes Mark did not actually think much of himself and he was very sensitive to rejection. He was envious of some of his other friends, whom he saw as having it easy, and this created arguments between them. Occasionally Mark would find himself rebounding between one group of friends and another, or else feeling that no-one really liked him and that he did not fit in anywhere. When he was down he would spend more time on his own, but that often left him feeling more isolated and depressed.

Mark had girlfriends from time to time. He could be very entertaining and people found him attractive. However, his insecurity soon started to surface and he would either become very jealous or else play things so 'cool' that people drifted away. In some ways he felt relieved when relationships ended, but this was soon replaced by familiar feelings of loneliness. At times he wondered what was 'wrong' with him and whether anything would change. Although he never acted on it, Mark occasionally felt that life was not worth living.

As in this example, when one problem leads to another it can be difficult for the person at the centre of it all to know where to start. For Mark, difficulties in one area tend to compound problems in another. For example, arguments at work might make it more likely for him to seek relief in drugs and alcohol, but this might well lead to more conflict at home. As he desperately tries to seek relief, so he steadily undermines the things that provide stability, putting him at risk of accumulating further problems. For many people with difficulties that 'interact' in this way, things can sometimes spiral into a state of crisis and it can then feel like a long journey back to the roots of the problem. For example, if Mark *had* begun to self-harm or even attempted suicide, then he may well have come into contact with psychiatric services of one kind or another. However, if he only ever accessed support at the point of crisis, then he might never really get to the heart of the problem.

Of course, the end results of a difficult childhood are by no means inevitable. For instance, it is not the case that everyone who has been abused in childhood turns to alcohol because of their experiences. Similarly, not everyone who uses drugs to cope with their feelings develops a psychiatric condition. Nevertheless, if these are some of the kinds of difficulties that you have been struggling with over the course of your life, then it may be particularly helpful at this point to try and make sense of them in terms of your reactions to previous experiences.

One aim of this book is to help someone in this situation to take the necessary first steps in taking a psychological approach to their problems without having to slide into a state of crisis first.

Adult development – the rest of the journey

Let us return to Erik Erikson's life-span model (Erikson 1950, 1959). We can use this to continue mapping out some of the ways in which childhood experiences carry over into adulthood.

In Part II, we ended our discussion at the fifth stage, that of *identity versus role confusion*. That stage normally occurs between the ages of 13 and 18 years. It is followed by the sixth stage, beginning in late adolescence.

The sixth stage – *intimacy versus isolation* – occurs roughly between the ages of 19 and 25 years. The aim is to branch out beyond the family and to begin to firmly establish oneself in the world as an individual. For instance, one goal is to begin to establish intimate relationships that go beyond adolescent 'infatuation'. If this stage goes well, then the person can expect to emerge with a certain amount of confidence about starting new friendships and taking on new challenges. Someone moving successfully through this stage will also have a sense of their family and friends being behind them as a 'safety net'. This is not to say that everything is likely to fall into place effortlessly for someone like this, but they might well have an optimistic sense of their own potential and a hopeful sense of the future. All being well, they will be able to *transfer* the sense of security they enjoyed in their family into their new relationships. They will find that they can trust other people appropriately and build up strong emotional bonds with them.

Difficulties at this stage might highlight underlying issues with trust. For example, someone who had struggled up to this point might feel stranded between new friends whom they do not yet quite fully trust and a family that may be unsupportive of their efforts to move on. This kind of 'push–pull' situation, in which there appears to be no middle ground, can be very challenging. It can leave the person feeling that they really have nowhere that feels safe. As a result, they might withdraw into themselves or else try to over-control their relationships by continually moving on and pushing people away. They might try to make a 'fresh start' again and again, in the hope that they can finally leave their insecurities behind. This strategy might help them to avoid getting hurt, but it can also lead them into a very lonely and isolated way of life.

The seventh stage – *generativity versus stagnation* – occurs roughly between 26 and 40 years of age. The challenge, during this lengthy stage, centres on the person's ability to manage and get on with others in the adult world. This includes their relationships and successes at home, at work and in social groups. The ideal is that this provides them with a real sense of achievement and personal well-being. Success at this stage might revolve around raising one's family or perhaps progressing in one's occupation or favourite pursuits. For others, a sense of 'generativity' and creativity might come from enjoying their relationships and from their ability to keep friends over long periods of time. All in all, it is about generally feeling *engaged* in a life that has meaning and that provides some satisfaction. Ideally, someone at this stage of life will also feel that they can contribute something to the world around them. Looking back over the years, they might be expected to feel that, overall, it has all been worth it – despite the ups and downs.

Of course, the flipside of this picture might be a longstanding sense of futility or boredom with life. For instance, if someone has spent much of their life on the sidelines, if their relationships have been disappointing and difficult and if they really do not feel that life has treated them fairly, then they are unlikely to feel particularly satisfied with how things have turned out. Instead, they may resent the progress that others have made and they may have many uncomfortable feelings of anger, envy and low self-esteem.

The final stage in this epic journey – *ego integrity versus despair* – occurs from around the age of 40 onwards. Briefly, this stage can be considered to revolve around self-acceptance. For instance, if someone has managed to pass more or less successfully through the preceding stages, then they would hopefully have an overall sense of satisfaction and acceptance. They might well feel that they are a generally 'well-rounded' individual. They might also be expected to enjoy a sense of acceptance of themselves and of the world around them during this, ideally, lengthy period. Following on from the last stage, they may have continued to find satisfaction in the things that have interested and inspired them. They will also have built up some good relationships along the way. If they have a family, they may also begin to see the fruit of their hard work and their dedication to their children as they continue to watch them grow and mature. Of course, there are many routes to achieving satisfaction by this stage in life, just as there are no absolutes or guaranteed recipes for happiness. The general aim is to achieve a feeling of contentment and satisfaction within one's own life story.

Alternatively, if things really have not gone well up to this point –
for whatever reason – then we can imagine that rather different
feelings will have set in over time. For instance, someone who enters
this stage of life deprived of a sense of achievement may now feel even
more embittered towards those whom they blame for their bad luck.
Equally, they may have felt that they had nothing to offer the world
and that they really deserved no better than they received in the end.
Either way, the overriding sense of negativity is likely to continue to
colour their outlook on life, whilst adding to their feelings of resentment and helplessness.

These examples are provided as a 'rough guide'. They provide an
outline sketch of how people's lives can turn out. Of course, the
variations are endless, so take a moment now to locate yourself on
this map. Where are you on this journey, and how would you say
things have turned out for you so far? Where will this take you?
Can you change course, and what do you feel you need to change
so that you have more chance of getting where you want to go?

10 Symptoms and diagnoses

Childhood sexual abuse, neglect and other kinds of emotional and physical trauma can increase the risk of the occurrence of a wide variety of symptoms, conditions and disorders. On the basis of the research evidence spanning the last 20 years or so, a broad range of problems have been linked to sexual abuse in childhood (Fergusson and Mullen 1999). These include:

- depression
- anxiety
- phobias
- Obsessive-Compulsive Disorder (OCD)
- Post-Traumatic Stress Disorder (PTSD)
- eating disorders
- dissociative disorders
- substance abuse and misuse
- suicide, attempted suicide, self-harm
- personality disorders.

Of course, this list is by no means exhaustive and there are many other important ways in which experiences of sexual abuse in childhood can influence your life as an adult. Furthermore, the problems that affect people in their everyday lives, sometimes for years on end, do not always fit neatly into the diagnostic 'boxes' used by professionals. However, it can be very useful to be familiar with some of the terms that are commonly used. This will help you to communicate with professionals to make sure that you get the best kind of care that is available.

Two of the main systems uses by healthcare professionals are the *Diagnostic and Statistical Manual of Mental Disorders* (DSM-IV-TR; APA 2000) and the *International Statistical Classification of Disease and Related Health Problems*, 10th Revision (ICD-10; World Health Organization 1993). Both provide comprehensive systems of classification for many of the difficulties people experience. As such, they provide a *common language* that is used internationally across a broad range of medical, legal, health and social care settings.

In this chapter there are brief definitions of the more commonly occurring conditions. This background information will help you in discussing your difficulties with your GP or a psychological therapist. Many of these terms have become a part of our everyday language and, as a result, the original meanings have become blurred. For this reason it is also worth doing what you can to make sure that you and any professional involved in your care are talking the same language from the outset. The diagnostic categories below are drawn from the DSM-IV-TR (APA 2000). Along with the ICD-10, this manual provides an invaluable framework for describing a broad range of symptoms and conditions. Although there are many possible causes for any particular condition, the list is made up of some of the more commonly occurring conditions that have also been related to childhood sexual abuse. Each condition is described in everyday terms as a way of breaking down the technical jargon that can sometimes be confusing and off-putting.

Depression

Depression, usually in the form of a depressive 'episode', is characterised by a period of at least two weeks during which time the person has suffered from a number of particular symptoms. Normally, these symptoms are severe enough so as to cause a marked change in the person's usual level of functioning. The main symptoms include depressed mood for most of the day as well as a loss of interest or pleasure in everyday activities. Changes in appetite are also common and can lead to unexpected weight loss or weight gain. People with depression are also likely to sleep a lot less than usual. However, the reverse can also be true and some depressed people tend to over-sleep instead. People with depression are also likely to feel agitated and irritable, or else to feel rather slowed down and sluggish because of their low mood. Anything and everything can seem like a big effort in the middle of a depressive episode.

Depression can also lead to physical symptoms, including aches and pains that appear to have no obvious physical cause. People with depression often find it difficult to concentrate or make decisions. They may see themselves as worthless and be overly self-critical. They may feel very guilty and, if the depression is severe, they can begin to experience suicidal thoughts and feelings.

The symptoms of depression can appear as a one-off episode or can come and go, leading to repeated episodes of severe depression with more settled (euthymic) periods in between. However, depression can also linger for many years in the form of a persistent low mood, sometimes referred to as Dysthymic Disorder. These chronic feelings are usually accompanied by other symptoms, such as feelings of low self-esteem and hopelessness.

Depression is usually accompanied by particularly bleak and negative thoughts about oneself, other people and the world in general. Depressed people tend to have little sense of optimism about the future and can feel quite hopeless about change. They may not feel like seeing other people and can become socially withdrawn. Sometimes this is because they do not feel that they have anything to offer and can see little point in being around other people. Being surrounded by others who do not seem depressed can also add to a sense of personal failure for some people, particularly in those whose depression is fuelled by feelings of guilt, shame or self-criticism.

Depression can set up a number of vicious circles in the person's everyday life. For instance, a depressed person may feel extremely tired and run down for much of the time. As a result, they can feel irritable and short-tempered, and friends and family may well view them as 'difficult'. However, self-imposed isolation can also add to their feelings of worthlessness and rejection, compounding the negative beliefs they might already hold about themselves and other people. The more they withdraw to protect themselves from the painful feelings of rejection, the more alone they can end up. Just finding the motivation to engage in psychological therapy can be a big hurdle for people who suffer from severe and enduring depression.

Anxiety

There are many anxiety-related disorders. These include Generalised Anxiety Disorder, Agoraphobia, Panic Attack, Panic Disorder, Phobia, Obsessive-Compulsive Disorder and Post-Traumatic Stress Disorder. The term 'anxiety' is frequently used in everyday language and the precise meaning can be lost when it is used in too general a way. It is useful to know some of the basic differences between these conditions, as there may be important differences in terms of what type of treatment is most suited to you.

Generalised Anxiety Disorder is characterised by excessive anxiety and worry. The person usually finds it difficult to control the worry and this may be accompanied by other symptoms such as restlessness, poor sleep and difficulties with concentration. Before a firm diagnosis can be made, the symptoms will usually have lasted for more than six months. The person's worry may be 'free-floating' and revolve around relatively minor day-to-day events. The focus of anxious and repetitive thinking (rumination) often shifts over time. The anxious person may notice that when one problem is 'solved', they soon begin to worry about something else.

People suffering with this kind of anxiety may find it very difficult to settle or to concentrate on anything for long. They may feel constantly on edge, irritable and physically and emotionally drained much of the time. This is partly because their sleep can be significantly affected, but also because they spend so much time thinking about the awful things that might happen that their mood eventually becomes quite low in the process.

People with this condition tend to have developed particular thinking styles based around 'thinking the worst' or 'catastrophising'. They may have a fatalistic outlook on life and have the idea that if they are not worried then there really is something to worry about, because something awful is bound to happen if they ever let up. Deeper beneath the surface they may also believe that worrying somehow prevents bad things from happening. This kind of belief can be a form of 'magical thinking', which occurs in childhood (Sugarman 1987). In therapy, it can be difficult to challenge if it has carried over into adulthood (Einstein 2006; Moulding 2006). Worrying then becomes a kind of 'safety behaviour', in that the person believes it helps them to cope with uncertainty. However, the price one pays for the false promise of certainty is being tied to worrying about one thing after another. If this pattern becomes too entrenched it can lead to other conditions such as Obsessive-Compulsive Disorder (OCD; Bolton *et al.* 2002). People who constantly worry about life in this way may also be tempted to seek reassurance from friends and family. However, reassurance never seems to work for very long. Seeking reassurance elicits sympathy from some, but it can easily stir up frustration and irritation in others over time.

Depending on its severity, people suffering from this kind of anxiety are also likely to find it difficult to manage very well in their everyday lives. The long-term effects of tension and worry can also lead to physical symptoms, such as twitching, restlessness, dizziness and a variety of digestive symptoms that do not have any obvious physical cause. Occasionally, people with these kinds of bodily – or somatic – symptoms find themselves repeatedly seeking reassurance that nothing is wrong with them from their GPs. As above, the reassurance rarely lasts long.

Phobia

A phobia is a more specific form of anxiety disorder. The phobic reaction occurs when the person is faced with the feared objects, places or situations. Common examples include animals, hypodermic needles, heights and enclosed spaces, but the list is potentially endless. People may also have more than one phobia. The phobic reaction can include a range of symptoms, including a pounding heart, sweating and rapid breathing. This is usually accompanied by negative and 'catastrophic' thoughts. The thoughts tend to centre on some awful consequence of being trapped with the feared object, such as fainting, losing control or being harmed in some way. Panic attacks can sometimes occur if the person believes that they cannot immediately escape from the feared object.

The phobic reaction can also be triggered by the anticipation of the feared object, leading to a chronic sense of dread. Understandably, this often leads people to avoid the feared object as much as possible. But, as with other anxiety disorders, further difficulties can arise from the over-use of avoidance to cope with the anxious feelings. If the consequences of the phobia begin to affect one's ability to function and to take part in everyday life, then it is worthwhile seeking treatment. Therapy is usually based around a programme of relaxation training combined with gradually increasing one's exposure to the feared object or situation. Of course, this is the opposite of avoidance, but if it is done in a systematic and careful way, the results are often good.

One form of phobia that deserves more exploration is Social Phobia. This is characterised by excessive fears about possible embarrassment or humiliation in a group. People with this type of phobia avoid situations where they believe they are likely to be scrutinised in any way. Usually this is because of an underlying fear of being judged negatively by others. Often the anticipation and dread of the situation is enough to make people avoid social situations wherever possible.

People who are already struggling with a sense of shame and stigma, perhaps because of events in their childhood, may well suffer with this kind of anxiety. Behind their discomfort with social situations, they may also fear being blamed or rejected if anyone were to find out more about them and their past.

In a severe form, this phobia can have a serious impact on one's everyday life. Understandably, this increases the risk of further problems. Treatment may take several forms, but if the underlying cause is childhood sexual abuse then it will be most important to explore the role of shame and stigma in fuelling any social phobia.

Obsessive-Compulsive Disorder (OCD)

OCD is another anxiety-based disorder. It is characterised by anxiety-provoking obsessions and by the compulsive actions that are performed in order to reduce the anxiety that results from the obsessional thoughts.

Obsessions generally take the form of disturbing thoughts, impulses or images. The person usually experiences these as intrusive and unwanted. Often, the more the person tries to push the thoughts from their mind, the more persistent they become. Sometimes the thoughts and images are experienced as abhorrent or as socially unacceptable, and the person fears losing control and acting on them for this reason. For example, they may contain violent or sexual imagery. They may also relate to aggressive fantasies. Other forms of obsession can relate to fears about losing control, being contaminated or coming to some other kind of harm *unless* things are in a specific order or *unless* certain actions are performed in a particular way.

The anxiety generated by the obsessive thoughts and images then drives the compulsions. For instance, someone who has obsessive fears about being 'contaminated' may try to deal with fear through excessive cleaning. Having done so, they may feel clean, safe and less anxious for a short while. However, the nature of OCD is that the obsessive feelings quickly build up again. Compulsions take many forms, but are usually some kind of repetitive or ritualised action. Examples include excessive hand washing, cleaning or checking electrical switches. However, they can just as easily be 'internal' actions, such as silent counting or the repetition of special words or phrases.

People who suffer from OCD may be very ashamed of their secret struggles and go to great lengths to conceal their ritualised behaviour from others. Naturally, this can create barriers between people and make people with OCD seem more difficult to reach. The role of OCD as a form of protection against interpersonal intimacy – especially if this is someone the person fears – also needs careful consideration because the disorder can lead to severe withdrawal and isolation.

Whatever the underlying reasons for the OCD in any particular case, a vicious circle quickly develops because the compulsive behaviours only tend to lead to temporary relief from the anxiety caused by the obsessional thoughts. Caught in a circular trap, someone with OCD can quickly develop extremely intricate and complex rituals for 'neutralising' or controlling the unwanted thoughts and images. In the most severe form, this can become all-consuming and the compulsions may be repeated every few minutes. At the other end of the spectrum, in a much milder form, it may mean going out of one's way every now and again to act upon the compulsions; for instance, occasionally turning back whilst on the journey to work to check that the cooker has been turned off or checking several times that the front door is locked.

People with OCD struggle to reassure themselves that things will be 'okay'. They may begin to seek this from friends, family and professionals alike and this can begin to affect the quality of their relationships. Once again, reassurance from others rarely lasts long. In addition, seeking reassurance can also become compulsive in its own right.

The severity of OCD can fluctuate over time, but it is generally recognised as a long-term condition that has to be managed by the individual over a long period of time. Because the thoughts and feelings can be so strong, letting go of the belief that 'neutralising' one's thoughts through the compulsive behaviour actually stops bad things happening can be especially difficult to undo. Progress in therapy can sometimes seem to quickly disappear, especially if the person comes under prolonged stress once again for whatever reason.

Treatment for OCD depends on its severity. Mild OCD can be successfully treated in much the same way as other mild anxiety disorders. For example, the person might be coached in relaxation techniques and then encouraged to gradually break down the compulsive behaviours one part at a time. Slowly but surely, the person hopefully comes to accept that bad things will not automatically happen when they stop repeating the compulsive behaviour.

More severe OCD requires more in-depth psychological therapy. This requires further understanding of the content and the emotional meaning of the imagery for that person. People suffering from OCD can also have a tendency to see themselves and the world in 'all-or-nothing' terms. Integrating 'good' *and* 'bad' feelings can then be a major task in therapy. Nevertheless, finding some emotional middle ground can be especially useful in the treatment of OCD. For example, the person with excessively violent obsessive imagery may come to realise that their fears of their own aggressive feelings and perhaps the aggressive feelings of others have been so difficult to deal with in the past that they have tried to split them off and push them away. Of course, none of us can control our thoughts or tidy up our emotions in this way and so the feelings inevitably stay with us – but disguised behind the symptoms of OCD. Taking the sting out of the imagery and seeing the underlying emotional meaning of the obsessive thoughts can also reduce the compulsive aspects of the OCD. Psychological therapy, which encourages the expression of difficult feelings in a *safe* way, can be very effective in reducing the frequency of the symptoms and identifying the triggers that can cause OCD to flare up.

Adults who have experienced sexual abuse as children can be especially prone to this condition (Lochner *et al.* 2002) because it revolves around the issue of control. If you felt invaded and disempowered as a child, then it may be all the more important to feel safe and secure as an adult. Similarly, if you have been exposed to sexual behaviour at a point in your life when it was impossible to make sense of it, then your normal adult sexual desires may feel extremely dangerous and threatening. OCD can seem like a way of putting these desires into 'quarantine' and holding them at arm's length. Sadly, the battle is only ever with oneself and people with OCD can spend a great deal of time keeping their fears at bay in what can turn out to be a potentially endless struggle.

Post-Traumatic Stress Disorder (PTSD)

PTSD is the result of witnessing or experiencing horrifying or disturbing events. The effects can be immediate or delayed, sometimes surfacing many years later when triggered by further trauma or stress. The symptoms that characterise the disorder fall into three categories:

- re-experiencing
- avoidance of reminders
- emotional distress when confronted with reminders.

People can re-experience traumatic events in flashbacks, nightmares or intrusive and unwanted memories. Flashbacks are memories that are so vivid that, for a moment, it feels as though the traumatic events are actually happening all over again. Understandably people go out of their way to avoid reminders and can become very distressed when they cannot avoid people, places or situations that remind them of the original trauma.

Since PTSD is such an important condition in terms of understanding the possible after-effects of childhood sexual abuse, it is explored in greater detail in the next chapter. It provides a good example for understanding how one's thoughts, feelings and behaviour can be interlinked in a very powerful way.

Childhood sexual abuse has also been linked to 'Complex PTSD' (McLean 2003). Complex PTSD is characterised by severe and chronic symptoms of PTSD that may last for many years and that begin to affect the individual in other ways over and above the symptoms of PTSD listed above (Herman 1992; Roth *et al.* 1997). For instance, Complex PTSD can lead to changes in the person's self-concept such that they feel intense guilt, shame and worthlessness. In addition, Complex PTSD can lead to major changes in relationships so that the person withdraws from the world and experiences extreme distrust and hostility towards others. Furthermore, Complex PTSD can give rise to additional conditions such as depression, hopelessness and dangerous self-harm behaviour. There is also an overlap between the symptoms of Complex PTSD and Borderline Personality Disorder (described below). Distinguishing between the two requires careful and thorough assessment.

Eating disorders

Eating disorders include Anorexia Nervosa and Bulimia Nervosa. Anorexia Nervosa is characterised by a preoccupation with losing weight that can become obsessive. People suffering from Anorexia Nervosa use a variety of methods in order to lose weight and to avoid weight gain. These methods can include excessive dieting, exercise, self-induced vomiting and laxatives. The physical effects upon one's body soon become significant and can include amenorrhea –the suspension of the normal menstrual cycle – and other conditions such as anaemia and osteoporosis. Severely restricted diets can also result in changes in one's thinking, which can affect decision-making and judgement. This is an especially dangerous side-effect since Anorexia Nervosa is usually accompanied by serious distortions in self-perception. Sufferers sometimes continue to perceive themselves as 'fat' despite drastic changes in their body shape. Unfortunately, the anxiety this stirs up can be temporarily relieved by further weight loss and, as a result, a vicious circle can quickly become established. The sense of achievement and control that can accompany further weight loss can begin to dominate, with very dangerous consequences. As times goes on, the sufferer's preoccupation with weight gain can also get stronger, rather than diminish, despite increasing weight loss.

The Body Mass Index (BMI) is a way of comparing both weight and height. A BMI of less than 17.5 is used as one guideline for making the diagnosis, along with a careful assessment of the other defining characteristics of the disorder. People with Anorexia Nervosa often lack insight into the condition and may steadfastly deny that there is a problem, sometimes despite serious medical concerns to the contrary.

Bulimia Nervosa is a related condition and also revolves around a preoccupation with avoiding weight gain. However, Bulimia Nervosa is characterised by a cycle of bingeing and purging behaviour. Bingeing means consuming, within a short period of time, significantly more than one would expect to eat in an average meal. Bingeing also tends to involve large amounts of the high-calorie foods that are usually excluded from the strict dieting that is also often part of the disorder. Bingeing can be triggered by stress, emotional upset or as a reaction against a previously overly restrictive dietary regime. The 'high' that results from the rapid intake of sugary food quickly gives way to the more familiar fears about having lost control and underlying worries about weight gain. This anxiety can trigger a range of behaviours, including vomiting and the misuse of laxatives, in order to purge the body of calories.

Someone with Bulimia Nervosa is caught in a dangerous trap in which they may find themselves veering between one destructive 'coping' strategy and another. Sadly, it is often the case that bingeing starts out as the solution to underlying emotional distress, but the resulting fear of weight gain then becomes another problem. Purging then becomes the solution to the bingeing but this, in turn, stirs up further anxiety as well as feelings of shame and guilt. These feelings can be difficult to deal with and can trigger further bingeing as a way of finding temporary relief. This can be a very difficult cycle to break. Furthermore, much of the behaviour tends to be done in secret and it can be very difficult for others to know that something is wrong until the condition is quite advanced.

The psychological factors behind eating disorders such as Anorexia Nervosa and Bulimia Nervosa can be many and varied. Childhood sexual abuse has been recognised as one risk factor in the development of eating disorders. Whatever the underlying trigger, some common themes include a preoccupation with control, specifically control over one's body. For instance, some people with an eating disorder try to 'disappear' in an attempt to avoid further abuse by starving themselves away to nothing. Likewise, if the abuse occurred during puberty, then it is possible that some children will have become anorexic as an attempt to avoid any further physical maturity, since they may have feared that this would attract more of the abuser's attention.

As always, rather than assuming that we *know* what lies behind the development of this type of disorder in each and every case, it is important to recognise that there may well be many different paths leading to the same place. Hence, in telling one's own story, it may be that the links between early abusive events and the development of an eating disorder later in life become clear in a way that has a uniquely personal meaning. Similarly, focusing on the dieting and restricting behaviour, whilst clearly important, is probably of more value once your own life story has been heard, since the emotional meaning of the symptoms are then more likely to become clear. This is another way in which an appropriate form of psychological therapy can play an important role in addressing the complex issues behind eating disorders.

Dissociative disorders and dissociation

Dissociative disorders result from a significant disturbance in the complex relationship between consciousness, memory and self-awareness. For instance, conditions such as Dissociative Amnesia are defined by the inability to remember major elements of one's own life history. Gaps in memory can relate to particular periods of the person's life or to particular aspects of certain events. Traumatic or disturbing memories are more likely to be kept out of conscious awareness in this way. By contrast, Depersonalisation Disorder is characterised by recurrent episodes of feeling detached from oneself and others. Both of these conditions can be a part of PTSD.

The term 'dissociation' refers more broadly to a feeling of being 'spaced out' or emotionally numb. It can be thought of as an ongoing state of shock in which the person feels slightly removed from what is going on around them. In this state, they may be emotionally unresponsive, forgetful and seem rather out of touch with the people around them. Dissociation can also come and go over time and may recur during periods of increased stress or emotional overload.

Mild states of dissociation are not unusual or problematic in and of themselves. For instance, many people describe a similar feeling when they are engrossed in a good book or a film. Some people have learnt to control the amount of dissociation they experience and might deliberately use it to distract themselves by thinking about some pleasant experiences, for instance, whilst at the dentist or having an injection. However, dissociation as a result of childhood sexual trauma can be much more problematic because it may be more difficult to control. For instance, if upsetting and painful things happened to you as a child, then you may have escaped from the reality of what was happening by losing yourself in a fantasy or a daydream just to help get you through the experience. If this 'emergency' strategy is over-used, it can become built into your way of coping with everyday life. The withdrawal and emotional numbing may provide temporary relief from anxiety or distress, but the price is a chronic sense of detachment from oneself and others. If this also causes unpredictable lapses in concentration and memory, then the cost rapidly begins to outweigh any benefits.

If dissociative symptoms are present as a result of childhood sexual abuse and trauma, it is very important to take into account the defensive – or protective – function they might serve. People dissociate because the things they have witnessed or experienced were too disturbing and overwhelming to deal with at the time. Dissociation can be thought of as an emergency measure, like an emotional pain-killer, which is triggered in order to protect the person from experiencing overwhelming feelings. In short, it is there for a reason, not by chance. Psychological therapy, which gently explores the function of the dissociative symptoms, can be useful in slowly allowing this kind of defensive barrier to be lifted (Sinason 2002). Of course, this needs to be done in a safe and careful way and within the context of a trusting relationship.

Substance abuse and misuse

A very broad range of substances can be misused. The most notorious are alcohol, nicotine, cannabis and other street drugs such as cocaine. However, shop-bought and prescription medication can also be misused. Typically, the substances that are misused, whatever their source, have some kind of sedating, pain-relieving or mood-enhancing effects.

Substances are 'abused' when the person continues to take them despite their obvious detrimental consequences. For example, someone abusing amphetamines may find themselves in situations where being 'high' is either irresponsible, dangerous or both. Their ability to work and function may start to suffer because of both the immediate and long-term effects of continued usage. The consequences may be obvious to others, but denied by the individual, and may include the steady accumulation of a number of social, physical and even legal problems.

Substance dependency is diagnosed when someone continues to use a drug in a habitual way that leads them to build up a tolerance to it. The person also suffers some form of withdrawal symptoms when they do not use it for some time. They then go out of their way to get more supplies. There may be obvious signs that using the drug is having detrimental effects in terms of their health and ability to cope with everyday life. If the person's withdrawal symptoms are so strong that they immediately take more of the drug to relieve them, then an addiction has been established. This can be difficult to break and professional support and intervention is always recommended.

The more general term of 'substance misuse' is also used when the use of substances is problematic in one way or another. The consequences may be seen in terms of the person's physical and emotional health. However, there may be additional effects upon the person's ability to work and function, to care for their children adequately and to manage their relationships.

The reasons behind repeated substance misuse can be many and varied. For example, it may be learnt from peers or be seen as an essential part of being a member of a particular social group. It can also be seen as a form of self-medication. For instance, if someone is repeatedly using a drug in order to 'cope' or just to feel okay, then this is very different from occasional or 'recreational' use.

In psychological therapy it is extremely important to consider *why* someone might be using substances in this way. For instance, trauma, substance misuse and dissociation (as described earlier) are often closely linked. This is because drugs and alcohol can be used to suppress anxiety, to shut out troubling memories and to mask a wide range of feelings related to the original trauma. By helping you to explore the links between all of these issues, psychological therapy can be one way to change this relationship. Insight and awareness can help to put a different perspective on one's drug use. For instance, coming to see that drowning one's feelings in alcohol is a form of self-punishment and slow suicide can be a major turning point.

Suicide, attempted suicide, self-harm and self-injury

It can be important to know the difference between different forms of self-damaging and self-destructive behaviour. For example, suicidal feelings can be expressed in terms of thoughts, ideas, fantasies and plans. This is often referred to as 'suicidal ideation'. Being able to talk openly with a suitable professional about suicidal thoughts and feelings can be a great relief, and doing so can actually reduce the likelihood that these thoughts will ever turn into actions. The act of suicide can be extremely impulsive; on the other hand, some people plan it out in great detail. Needless to say, whilst thinking and talking about suicide in no way means that it is bound to happen, these feelings should always be considered with the greatest caution and concern because there is always an element of risk attached. Unfortunately, it can be very difficult to predict who is at risk of actually turning such thoughts into action. For some people, suicidal feelings can only be contained and survived given a period of appropriate medication and hospitalisation. For others, it is the provision of a safe relationship with a professional in which they can explore their feelings without causing undue panic that is most helpful.

Deliberate acts of self-harm and self-injury can also reflect a wide range of feelings and impulses. There is also an infinite number of ways in which people can hurt themselves. This might include cutting or burning one's own body, but it may also include taking unnecessary risks, not looking after oneself properly in terms of diet or healthcare, or repeatedly putting oneself in a position where one is likely to be mistreated by others.

For some people, self-harm can be an attack upon themselves because they feel that they are worthless, bad or guilty in some way. For other people, it represents a veiled attack on others and an expression of the hidden anger and frustration that the person may be too afraid to express in any other way. Additionally, some people who self-harm describe it as a way of allowing themselves to feel 'something'.

Once again, it would be unwise to assume that it is possible to know from the outset just what these behaviours mean to any particular individual. Psychological therapy can be helpful here, but its success depends greatly upon the person's motivation and upon them making a decision, at some level, that they want to change their behaviour. Naturally, understanding the emotional difficulties behind self-harming behaviour can be especially important. As with suicidal thoughts and feelings, there is always an element of risk attached to self-harm. Accidents can easily happen and things can quickly go wrong. If this is the way that you have found to 'cope' with your feelings, then addressing it openly and honestly in a safe setting is a priority because the risks and possible consequences cannot be ignored.

Personality disorders

Receiving a diagnosis of Personality Disorder can be especially difficult. The term itself is very broad and has been much misunderstood and misused. To add to the confusion, different people sometimes use and interpret the term 'Personality Disorder' in very different ways. Like others, the term has also suffered through overgeneralisation and has found its way into the public consciousness, but often without sufficient explanation or understanding. At worst the term has become a kind of shorthand for 'dangerous' or 'untreatable'. Because Personality Disorder is an umbrella term for a very wide range of personality types, inaccurate and inconsistent use of the term continues to cause unnecessary confusion and upset.

The *Diagnostic and Statistical Manual of Mental Disorders* (DSM-IV-TR; APA 2000) lists ten specific personality disorders. They differ from each other in very important ways. Because the descriptions of each disorder are so detailed, they allow several different aspects of a person's character and behaviour to be seen as part of a bigger picture. Because the person suffering from a Personality Disorder is likely to have difficulties that are long-standing and deep-seated, the term allows us to start to think about the way in which different aspects of a person's character combine and continue to create problems for them. Because one problem area is often linked to another, it can be difficult to achieve lasting improvement by only focusing on one problem or another without seeing how things link up. Effective treatment needs to be well thought out, systematic and therefore usually a long-term prospect.

Childhood sexual abuse has been associated with a number of personality disorders (Johnson *et al.* 2003). In particular, the possible relationship between childhood sexual abuse and Borderline Personality Disorder has received a lot of attention over the years (Ogata *et al.* 1990; Silk *et al.* 1995). This particular diagnosis will be explored in more detail in chapter 14, because it also has links with more severe and complicated forms of PTSD, described above as Complex PTSD.

For now, it is important to have an overview of the key features of Borderline Personality Disorder. These include difficulties with mood that can lead to intense feelings, such as anger and anxiety, that are difficult to manage. The intensity of the feelings might lead to frequent fights or angry outbursts that seem impossible to control at the time. Under stress, the person may also feel paranoid or begin to dissociate. There can be difficulties with controlling one's behaviour, leading to impulsive and potentially dangerous actions, including self-harm or attempted suicide. People with Borderline Personality Disorder also struggle with their sense of identity and can often feel fragmented and chaotic. Their relationships tend to suffer greatly because of this and they can react to rejection in extreme and destructive ways. Behind the frequent 'crises' and turmoil in their lives, they may feel quite empty and desperate. These feelings can lead to substance misuse problems, which inevitably make things worse in the long run.

11 Focus on Post-Traumatic Stress Disorder

Post-Traumatic Stress Disorder, or PTSD, is a 'reactive' disorder. In other words, it develops as a response to experiencing (one or many) traumatic events that are both frightening and overwhelming. Anyone can suffer from PTSD. The likelihood of someone developing the disorder in a particular set of circumstances depends upon many factors. However, the basic elements are that the person experienced something that seriously threatened their life or their physical well-being in some way. Their reaction, understandably, is expected to have involved extreme feelings of fear and helplessness. Of course, the event could have been a one-off incident or something that happened many times. People can also suffer from PTSD after witnessing dreadful things happening to other people. PTSD can be mild, moderate or severe.

There are a number of symptoms that can result from this kind of experience. These include:

- Re-experiencing the event – perhaps in the form of intrusive images, recurrent dreams or flashbacks of the event.
- Attempts to avoid reminders of the event – such as trying not to think about what happened or avoiding people and places that act as reminders.
- Persistent symptoms of heightened arousal – such as difficulties with concentration, problems getting to sleep and increased anxiety.

The diagnosis of PTSD was first introduced into the *Diagnostic and Statistical Manual of Mental Disorders* in 1980 (APA 1980). Before this, similar patterns and clusters of symptoms were described using other terms, such as 'shell shock' or 'battle fatigue'. Whilst previous attention has centred upon the symptoms that are more likely to result from exposure to the horrors of the battlefield, the concept of PTSD can be applied to any kind of situation in which a person has been overwhelmed by frightening and disturbing experiences. Whereas adults react with obvious signs of fear or horror, children might show their distress in other ways, such as through disturbed behaviour. PTSD can also occur at any age, and the symptoms might appear straightaway or after a delay, sometimes of several years. Symptoms can come and go over the course of one's life, but may be more likely to reappear during stressful periods or in the wake of a more recent trauma. When the symptoms of PTSD are so enduring and severe as to lead to other problems, the term 'Complex PTSD' is often used (Herman 1992; Hegadoren *et al.* 2006). Examples of additional difficulties associated with Complex PTSD include depression, changes in self-concept and an increase in suicidal and self-harming behaviour.

As well as providing a diagnosis – which can help to identify an appropriate course of treatment – the concept of PTSD is also invaluable because it provides a framework within which to understand our responses to traumatic events. By and large, the characteristic responses are universal, and it is clear from the wealth of evidence and research literature that PTSD can affect *anyone*. Using the term 'PTSD' to explain the wide variety of symptoms that can result from childhood sexual abuse can be especially useful in psychological therapy. This is because it can give a name to the seeming jumble of feelings and symptoms that the person has been experiencing. It also provides an explanation for why the symptoms have developed and why they might have persisted over time. These insights are often a good starting point in therapy, because they help us to see that anyone could have developed the symptoms if they had been through equally traumatic experiences themselves. It is important to appreciate that developing PTSD is not a sign of weakness, nor does it indicate a flaw in one's character. Instead, it is a reflection of the traumatic nature of the event itself.

Childhood sexual abuse can be traumatic, not only because it might be accompanied by threatened or actual violence, but also because it can provoke feelings of fear, helplessness and horror. Of course, it can also produce feelings of disgust and shame. Over time, these feelings can evolve into depression or other difficulties associated with low self-esteem, in addition to the original symptoms of PTSD.

For some people the symptoms of PTSD gradually disappear over time, but for others the symptoms can persist unchecked for many years (Resnick *et al.* 1993; Ehlers and Clark 2000). The symptoms last because traumatic events, of any kind, can set in place a powerful chain-reaction between the following:

- thoughts
- feelings
- behaviours.

Because the relationship between these three areas can vary considerably from one person to another, it is very helpful to consider how they might be linked in one's own case and how they might work together to maintain one's symptoms. Trauma-focused psychological therapy can be especially useful for exploring and then breaking these links. The process will be discussed in more detail in Part IV, but for now it is important to have a general understanding of PTSD and the way in which it leads to particular symptoms.

Because our thoughts, feelings and behaviours are so interlinked, certain patterns emerge when we experience a significant threat to our safety or sense of well-being. For instance, if we think we are in danger, our bodies react physically, and this produces certain feelings and sensations. These feelings typically trigger particular kinds of behaviours that are designed to help us deal with the threat in one way or another.

This type of chain-reaction is often referred to as the 'fight or flight' response. It is triggered off in everyday situations, such as when a car pulls out in front of you unexpectedly or when the phone rings late at night. In this kind of situation you might feel startled for a moment, but the feeling usually settles after a short while. This is especially so if you are able to reassure yourself that there is no emergency after all and that you are not in any immediate danger. By contrast, people who have been traumatised are more likely to be very sensitive to any sense of danger. They might have adopted an approach to the world based on the belief that 'it is always better to be safe than sorry'. As a result, one problem is that they are then more likely to see potential threats where there may be none, and to react accordingly. They might also be quite jumpy and irritable around other people because their nerves are constantly 'on edge'. If this is the case, other people are more likely to perceive them as awkward and 'prickly' and so keep their distance. If this just leaves the individual feeling rejected and misunderstood, then it can compound their negative feelings about themselves.

Case example – Anna

Anna started to develop some PTSD-type symptoms soon after her stepfather had begun to come into her room and sexually abuse her. For

on after childhood sexual abuse*

example, she had difficulty sleeping and began to have nightmares about people breaking into the house. She became very wary of her stepfather and would never stay in the same room as him during the day.

Anna also began to withdraw from other people. She stopped going out and gave up her favourite activities of swimming and cycling with her friends. Instead, she preferred to stay at home to be around her mother. Her mother noticed how 'clingy' she had become, but put this down to her worries about going to secondary school.

Partly because of a lack of sleep, Anna became more irritable and impatient with other people. She became frustrated very easily and did not seem able to concentrate on anything for long. Previously, Anna had been able to absorb herself in play for hours on end, but now she seemed constantly 'on edge'. She did not seem to settle at anything and she easily tired of things. Her teacher began to notice that her homework was often late and hastily done.

Because Anna's mother did not understand what was happening, she became increasingly critical of her daughter. She tired of her moodiness and unpredictable temper. Out of frustration, she began to tell her to 'grow up' and to stop being a 'mummy's girl'. This made Anna feel quite helpless and, instead of being able to express this any other way, she became angry and began to blame her mother for being 'useless'.

As in this example, it is easy to see how rapidly vicious circles can build up for someone with PTSD. Furthermore, if the people around them misread the symptoms, then children like Anna can also find themselves being blamed for being 'difficult' or under-performing at school. The cause of the original difficulties can then become increasingly difficult to recognise.

At this point we will spend some more time looking at what happens in each of the key areas of thoughts, feelings and behaviour.

Thoughts

The trauma caused by childhood sexual abuse tends to lead to the development of particular thoughts and beliefs. In order to try and make sense of what is happening to them, children can quickly take on some very negative assumptions about themselves and about the world around them. These assumptions can become more entrenched over time. For example, having been abused, some children may come to believe that 'nowhere is safe' or that other people somehow sense that they are 'a victim'. Some children begin to believe that they 'deserved bad things to happen to them' and that people 'will *always* treat them badly'. It is understandable that if awful things have continued to happen to them over the course of their childhood, then their pessimistic assumptions about life are unlikely to change.

The explanations children come up with in order to try to understand their experiences will be influenced by the developmental stage they are at when the abuse occurs. For example, younger children may be more likely to believe that *no-one* can be trusted. Older children may be more likely to feel deeply ashamed of their sexuality and to be painfully aware of their 'difference' to other children of their own age.

Trauma can also affect one's memory. This can sometimes make it more difficult to think about and make sense of the past. Because our ability to remember particular events depends partly on the state of mind we were in at the time, a traumatic event can be stored in a fragmented way. This can mean that it is difficult to tell the story of what happened from beginning to end because the fragments do not seem to fit together (Siegel 1995). In some cases, especially when the person has very few clear memories of the past, they can be left in a state of confusion and uncertainty along with a nagging sense that 'something' is wrong. However, the more difficult it is to clearly remember specific events, the more difficult it becomes to focus on them in therapy.

False Memory Syndrome was discussed in Part I of this book. With this in mind, it is essential to recognise that having only a vague memory of one's childhood, suffering from anxiety and even having bad dreams does *not* prove or disprove that one has a history of childhood sexual abuse. Similar groups of symptoms can develop for all kinds of reasons. For example, growing up in a household where there was significant parental conflict or experiencing frequent moves can have similar effects. Suffering the unexpected loss of a close family member or coping with serious physical illness in childhood can also lead to similar patterns of symptoms. The same can be said of many other unpredictable and troubling events. If you are someone who suspects that you were abused in childhood mainly because you have a sense that something bad happened, then psychological therapy may be more difficult and complicated for you. Because of this, any psychological therapy you undertake will need to be based on the clear understanding that both client and therapist may well never really 'know' what took place. In these circumstances, it is recommended that you proceed with extreme caution before jumping to any conclusions about what might be causing your current difficulties. However, it is possible to do useful work on the feelings of uncertainty and distrust that may have lingered on from childhood whilst avoiding the burden of having to 'prove' whether or not particular events took place. Those hoping to uncover a hidden memory that leads to everything in their past suddenly 'making sense' are unlikely to get this result using conventional psychological therapy, especially if they enter into it with that particular goal in mind.

For others, the memories of past trauma can be very vivid. The images can seem intrusive and appear to come out of the blue despite one's attempts to 'forget'. Whilst this can be distressing and unsettling, having clear memories of the past is helpful in therapy, as we shall see in Part IV.

Feelings

People who have experienced a traumatic event often remain very sensitive to the threat of similar things happening again. In other words they are 'on the lookout' for signs of a repeat. They are often hyper-aware of their environment, since they believe that bad things are more likely to happen to them. Using the example of a car crash survivor, this kind of intense watchfulness or 'hyper-vigilance' might lead them to drive in an edgy and anxious way whilst constantly scanning for the next car to pull out on them unexpectedly. Being in the car, travelling at speed or approaching a particular junction can all act as signs of imminent threat, which can then trigger the 'fight or flight' response.

Once this happens, the person's body reacts by releasing hormones such as adrenalin. This has a number of powerful physical effects because it is preparing the body for immediate physical action. Adrenalin automatically causes your heart rate to increase and can make your heart feel as if it is thumping loudly in your chest. Your breathing rate also increases, sometimes leading to the sensation of a shortness of breath because your breathing becomes fast and shallow. Blood then rushes to the muscles of the arms and legs in preparation for physical action, which can lead to the familiar sensation of 'jelly legs'. Blood also rushes away from the other organs, such as the stomach, which can lead to an unsettling 'butterflies' in the stomach feeling. Because the rate of breathing increases, the balance of oxygen and carbon dioxide in the bloodstream also begins to change. Once this happens, your ability to think clearly and to make decisions can also alter. Of course, this makes judging situations accurately even more difficult.

Quite often people who suffer from frequent anxiety attacks also tend to interpret the physical effects of adrenalin as proof that they really are in danger. Unfortunately, this leads to even greater levels of adrenalin being released. For example, some people interpret the physical sensations of anxiety as a sign that they are having a heart attack or going 'mad'. Of course, these are disturbing thoughts in their own right, which can lead to a spiral of further anxiety because the person perceives yet more threat – this time from inside themselves. This kind of rapidly escalating anxiety can sometimes lead to a panic attack, which can feel extremely disorientating and unsettling. Unfortunately, once such a pattern has been established, the person can be so fearful of having another panic attack that they withdraw even more in an attempt to avoid any possible triggers to these unpleasant symptoms. We learn very quickly when we are frightened. Psychological therapy following trauma is a process of loosening up some of the hard-and-fast ideas that have developed in the wake of the traumatic experience.

Having experienced the raw feelings that accompany the fight or flight response, the person can be left feeling embarrassed and drained. They might also feel ashamed that they continue to have these anxious feelings as an adult. If these symptoms were the result of sexual trauma in childhood, angry feelings about the unfairness of continuing to suffer can be stirred up. The ongoing effects of early trauma are like throwing a pebble into a pool; the ripples and waves carry on spreading out and can influence many areas of one's life.

Naturally, not everyone responds to the fight or flight reaction in the same way. For example, some people get a very dry mouth and others feel nauseous, whereas some people tend to feel dizzy or 'spaced out'. Other people describe feeling as if their thoughts are racing, whilst many just tend to notice a pounding sensation in their chest. Whatever your own particular reaction, the fight or flight response can be very powerful and unsettling. There are many ways of masking or suppressing these feelings, some of which are more harmful in the long term than others. For example, smoking can give the person the feeling that their anxiety has subsided, as can drinking alcohol. Of course, the long-term risks of both are well known. Prescription medication is often used to help people to take the edge off anxiety. Different types and dosages of medication will be associated with different levels of relaxation and sedation, and each will have different kinds of side effects. The general recommendation for medication that reduces anxiety is that it is best used only as a short-term treatment. Fortunately, there are many other ways to reduce anxiety.

Many people use anxiety management techniques such as relaxation training or meditation. Regular exercise and activities such as yoga can be useful too. If you suffer from anxiety on a frequent basis, then it is worth taking the time to find something that suits you without becoming an additional burden in its own right. However, it is also important to recognise that the fight or flight response is a natural part of life. It is there to help us respond to danger when we need to and it can be a lifesaver.

Behaviour

Because the effects of the fight or flight response can be so unwelcome and so unpleasant, people naturally tend to find ways to avoid the situations that cause the anxiety. Avoidance is closely linked with PTSD and can be difficult to overcome, especially if it has been overused as a way of coping.

Avoidance *works* because our anxiety begins to subside once we get away from the immediate 'threat'. This provides an instant pay off. However, the long-term use of avoidance has the opposite effect because it just tends to reinforce rather than reduce our sense of danger.

Clearly, if there is a situation that is obviously dangerous, then it is only natural to try to steer well clear. But if avoidance is something you do more often than not, it can become counter-productive. Avoidance can occur in any area of one's life and the variations are infinite. For example, it can mean turning down invitations from friends because of fears about meeting new people or being in a crowd. It could mean avoiding becoming more deeply involved with a current partner because of hidden fears of dependency in relationships. It might also mean avoiding having a healthy and enjoyable sex life because of feelings of shame about one's own body and sexuality.

Psychological therapy for the after-effects of trauma is usually based upon exploring and understanding how these three aspects – thoughts, feelings and behaviour – work together. The first step is to begin to build up the picture of how one thing leads to another in your own case. Once you can see how the chain reaction works, you can begin to break the cycle.

Thought–feeling–behaviour chains

For someone who has experienced childhood sexual abuse, the triggers to the fight or flight response can be many and varied.

Particular places, certain sights, smells, aspects of other people's appearance and all kinds of situations can act as triggers to the sense of being in danger once again. This often happens within seconds and the fight or flight response can be quickly triggered, leading to the chain reaction described above. Since the effects of adrenalin can be so unpleasant, it is understandable that people will go out of their way to avoid people, places or anything that reminds them of the traumatic events in any way.

People with a traumatic past also often try to push reminders of the events out of their mind. Since none of us can actually control our thoughts like this for any length of time, attempts to push the thoughts away can leave you feeling defeated. This sense of being trapped with the symptoms can sometimes lead to more drastic attempts to avoid reminders of the past. People with PTSD sometimes turn to drugs and alcohol in order to dull the senses and to create a temporary sense of control and relief (Ouimette and Brown 2003). This is another form of 'avoidance', since the feelings are not being faced; instead, they are being masked and deadened. So long as the cycle of threat, anxiety and avoidance (in whatever form it takes) is repeated, the more entrenched the pattern becomes and the less likely things are to change by themselves.

However, once you can make the connection between these thoughts, feelings and behaviours, then you can begin to turn things around. For instance, if you find that relaxation or some form of anxiety management works for you, then you will increase your chances of being able to reduce your reliance upon avoidance. So, whilst it is important to see how these things can spiral downwards, it is even more important to see how small changes can often help to break up the chain reaction.

PTSD in children

Children are more likely to show the effects of recent trauma through their behaviour and through anxiety-related symptoms. Depending on their age, this is partly because they are less likely to have the language to describe what they are feeling. In some cases children express their feelings through repetitive play, which re-enacts the traumatic scenario in some way. For example, their play may be overtly sexualised and they might use their toys to vividly re-enact what they have seen or experienced. Similarly, they might suffer from frequent and recurrent nightmares or bad dreams that are, in some way, associated with their experiences. Children can also express their distress through various physical – or somatic – symptoms, such as headaches and stomach-aches.

The diagnosis of PTSD can also be more difficult with children, because, as we have seen in Part II, the traumatic events occur during the process of such rapid development. This makes it more difficult to establish a clear picture of the child's functioning before the trauma for comparison, because so many things are in flux during childhood (Foa and Meadows 1997).

However, a sample of US-based surveys suggests a prevalence rate of PTSD of between 6 and 10 per cent in children (Giaconia *et al.* 1995; Kessler *et al.* 1995). A similar rate of between 4 and 8 per cent has been found in adults (APA 2000, p. 466; Narrow *et al.* 2002). Of course, a very wide range of events can lead to PTSD. However, childhood sexual abuse has been identified as a risk factor in the development of PTSD in adults (Roth *et al.* 1997).

12 Focus on Personality Disorder

As described previously, personality disorders are serious, long-term conditions that can affect many areas of an individual's life. Links have been found between childhood neglect and abuse and a number of different types of Personality Disorder. Examples of these include Avoidant Personality Disorder, Antisocial Personality Disorder and Dependent Personality Disorder (Johnson J.G. *et al.* 2000; Johnson D.M. *et al.* 2003). Childhood sexual abuse has also been linked to Borderline Personality Disorder in many studies (Ogata *et al.* 1990; Silk *et al.* 1995). However, it is important to recognise that not everyone who has a Personality Disorder has been abused and that childhood sexual abuse does not *automatically* lead to these kinds of difficulties (Fossati *et al.* 1999). A full list of the personality disorders and a detailed description of them from a psychiatric perspective can be found in the *Diagnostic and Statistical Manual of Mental Disorders* (APA 1980). Similarly, a more experiential and interpersonal description can be found in the *Psychodynamic Diagnostic Manual* (PDM Task Force 2006).

Personality disorders can be the result of a combination of particularly destructive and damaging early experiences. For example, chaotic relationships at home, poor parenting and frequent upheaval can be contributory factors. An atmosphere of neglect, including physical, emotional and sexual abuse, can also increase the risk of developing personality difficulties in later life. In general, it is important to remember that there are many possible causes of these conditions and that a combination of factors is often involved. In many cases, childhood sexual abuse may well be only one of the factors.

In this chapter we will explore Borderline Personality Disorder (BPD) in more detail. This condition affects people in a number of important ways. For example, people diagnosed with this condition usually have a long history of problems in many, if not all, of the following areas:

- mood
- impulse control
- relationships
- identity
- vulnerability to stress.

Mood

People with BPD often experience dramatic shifts in their moods. These shifts can be triggered by events in relationships and can include bouts of extreme anger. Prolonged periods of anxiety and depressed mood can also be a major feature, but these can give way to other uncomfortable feelings such as panic or despair. It can seem to other people that someone with BPD is always in a state of 'crisis' of one sort or another. A sense of relentless instability and emotional upheaval is a consistent aspect of the disorder. Behind the drama and chaos, people with BPD often complain of feeling terribly alone and empty. By contrast, some people with these difficulties may try to manage their feelings by becoming overly restrained and reserved. In some cases this emotional 'restriction' can be as marked as the 'outbursts' of others suffering with BPD.

Impulse control

Poor impulse control means that people find it difficult to contain their feelings. Instead, they tend to act on them and to make quick decisions based more on how they feel than on careful consideration of what is right for them in the long run. This can apply to all sorts of behaviour such as gambling, driving dangerously, binge drinking and unsafe sex. There is usually an element of risk to these behaviours. Because someone with BPD frequently experiences intense feelings, they can be more likely to resort to acts of self-harm or to attempt suicide.

Relationships

People with BPD tend to really struggle with close relationships. This is partly because they tend to see other people in their life in rather extreme ways. For instance, some people are seen as 'all good', whilst others are seen as 'all bad'. People with BPD tend to start relationships on a high and can often idealise new partners or acquaintances. This soon gives way to the other extreme and people can then be seen as deceitful and completely untrustworthy. Such sharp swings from one extreme to the other can be very difficult for the individual to cope with and, understandably, their partners and friends can really struggle to deal with the fallout.

In particular, relationships may be marked by desperate attempts on the part of the person with BPD to avoid being rejected or abandoned. This can lead to some extreme behaviour and to dangerous 'acting-out', such as threatening to kill oneself if a partner leaves. Such gestures and threats inevitably create more tension.

Identity

People suffering from BPD can feel very fragmented and insecure. It is as if they do not have a firm foundation in terms of who they are. As a result they can sometimes make sudden changes to their appearance or to their lifestyle as a whole. They can suddenly decide to set off on a whole new direction in life without any planning or forethought. The result is that they can struggle to hold down relationships at home and at work. They may 'move on' frequently and so never really manage to settle down at all. In the end the feelings of emptiness and of having nowhere to 'belong' can catch up, with serious consequences.

Vulnerability to stress

Of course, everyone is vulnerable to stress, but people with BPD tend to react in more extreme ways. In particular, they can become paranoid and extremely insecure. This might be accompanied by feelings of dissociation or being out of touch with reality. At these points, it might feel as if everything has just become too much to deal with. Although these episodes rarely last long they can be very disruptive and extremely unsettling.

In considering all of these features, it is important to recognise that BPD is about 'extremes'. For instance, everybody's moods fluctuate from day to day, and we are all vulnerable to over-react under stress now and again. By contrast, BPD describes a way of being that is longstanding and deep-seated. More often than not, the symptoms are extreme and disruptive. The fallout can significantly affect friends and family, as well as the person struggling to cope in the centre of it all. The difficulties described above can often show little tendency to change over time and problems usually continue to build up for someone with BPD. Although the diagnosis can be very difficult to receive, it must also be seen, for some people, as the potential starting point for making serious changes.

Case example – Kerry

Kerry's parents had experienced violence, abuse and neglect as children. They were struggling to cope and both relied heavily on alcohol. Home life for Kerry could be chaotic and very frightening. Her father had a violent temper and there were many times that Kerry witnessed domestic violence between her parents. Occasionally, her father would lash out at the children, and Kerry's teachers had noticed marks on her face and body that suggested she had been hit.

Kerry's mother also had a quick temper, and she would sometimes scream at the children, telling them that she did not want them and that it was 'all their fault'. To make up for this, she would then try to 'spoil' them with toys and gifts that, in reality, she could not afford. Because she felt so guilty, she would also promise not to shout at them again, but the peace never seemed to last for long. Later, when her mother began to become very depressed, Kerry saw her cut her wrist with a knife. Because Kerry was so young, she did not understand what was happening.

Kerry found it difficult to know where she was with her parents from one moment to the next. She became very withdrawn, but she could also have extreme temper tantrums. This caused more arguments and disruption at home because her parents often blamed each other for any difficulties their children were having.

Social Services became involved as a result of Kerry's teacher's concerns and neighbours' reports of constant shouting and arguing. Despite it being clear that her parents were struggling to cope, they were both very reluctant to consider allowing their children to go into care, even for respite. Eventually, Social Services were forced to take action and Kerry spent much of her childhood in and out of care, and in various foster homes.

When she came home, things would be settled for a while, but this would not last long and Kerry and her siblings would be removed once again. Kerry experienced sexual abuse by a carer during one of these periods in care. She was 7 years old and had some idea that this was wrong, but she did not know who to turn to. In any case, her life was so chaotic she did not want to cause any more trouble.

Kerry found it very hard to mix with other children. She could be moody and unpredictable, and she always seemed to prefer her own company. She tended to latch on to one carer or another, and then become very clingy. Kerry found it extremely difficult when a person she had become attached to spent time with other people. She would 'play up' to get attention, but this sometimes landed her in trouble. From time to time she seemed to have decided that she did not need anyone anyway, and she would angrily reject any attempts to comfort her.

Kerry left school and spent much of her time out of work. She found it difficult to settle anywhere and she did not really know what she wanted to do. She struggled in her relationships and sometimes believed that she was 'obsessed' with people. Invariably they seemed to let her down. On more than one occasion she physically attacked a young woman who she believed was making a move on her boyfriend. Eventually she was charged with assault.

Kerry had started drinking at an early age. She had also used solvents and cannabis. Sometimes she just wanted to reach a state of oblivion, and she had a reputation amongst her friends for not knowing when to stop. Since the age of fifteen she had also self-harmed. This seemed to come out of the blue, and she could not explain to others why she did it. She had begun by just scratching at her arms, but she moved on to use a razor blade to make deeper cuts. On several occasions she had gone to Accident and Emergency to have the wounds cleaned and stitched up.

The next time this happened, Kerry turned up in a very confused state. She had been drinking and smoking cannabis. She seemed very paranoid and believed that she had done something awful that meant she had to die. Kerry was admitted for assessment and after a few weeks she settled enough to go home. It was during this stay in hospital that she was diagnosed as having Borderline Personality Disorder. At first Kerry did not understand what this meant and it took some time with her keyworker to talk this through in detail. Kerry entered a groupwork programme provided by the hospital to help her to begin to manage her condition. The aim was simply to provide more information on the disorder and to help her understand how it was likely to affect her mood and her relationships. Just having more information was a start. The group leaders emphasised that making changes would be a long-term job and encouraged Kerry to tackle some of her immediate problems. She began to see a counsellor to help with her alcohol problem and slowly began to achieve some more balance in her life.

With support, and by taking small but steady steps to change things, Kerry was able to stay out of hospital and begin to put a life together for herself.

In this example, Kerry shows many of the signs of having **BPD**. A very unfortunate start in life had damaging long-term effects upon her development as an individual. Sexual abuse was clearly a very serious factor for her, but it happened in the midst of a host of other problems. For Kerry, early relationships were a major source of pain and distress, and these issues are often the focus of long-term psychological treatment for BPD. It is important to consider how all of these factors combined to create a very damaging environment for someone like Kerry. It would be less helpful to isolate any one aspect of her upbringing as being the key. Careful assessment and consideration of the diagnosis of BPD can act as a starting point for sketching out a long-term approach to change. For Kerry it began with understanding her diagnosis and then moving on to tackle her use of alcohol. Ideally, this will get her into a better place from which to continue thinking about the way ahead.

Borderline Personality Disorder and Complex Post-Traumatic Stress Disorder

In the last chapter we explored Post-Traumatic Stress Disorder (PTSD) in depth. When the effects of PTSD are particularly severe and chronic, they can lead to additional problems. These were described in the last chapter as 'Complex PTSD'. Symptoms include long-lasting changes in self-concept, intense feelings of guilt and shame and an increased risk of suicidal and self-harming behaviour. Other difficulties can include depression, extreme distrust, hostility and withdrawal from others.

There are some clear similarities between these symptoms and Borderline Personality Disorder (Herman 1992; McLean 2003). Because of these similarities, there is a risk of misdiagnosis. This can have implications for the kind of treatment that is suggested to you. Getting a good assessment and having a good understanding of any diagnosis you receive is therefore extremely important. This will help you to look into the condition in more detail and to help yourself to get the right kind of treatment and support. Becoming familiar with these conditions, and the possible overlap between them, will also help you to engage in the assessment process and to get the most out of it.

There are many helpful sources of further information on BPD that you can access through some of the websites listed under 'General health and mental health advice' in the Further Information, Links and Contacts section at the back of the book. Many of the websites also provide recommended book lists. A good example of a self-help book for BPD is *Managing Intense Emotions and Overcoming Self-Destructive Habits* by Lorraine Bell (2003).

13 Putting it all together: a joined-up approach

Multiple symptoms and everyday life

Of course, real life is often far less straightforward than any list of symptoms might suggest. Inevitably there will be overlaps between different conditions, and developing one condition can lead to an increased risk of developing another. An example is someone struggling with depression, but who has relied on alcohol to lift their mood. When one condition exists alongside another, they are described as being 'co-morbid'. This can make treatment more complicated, and will be discussed in more detail in Part IV. For now, it is important to appreciate that when one problem exists alongside another, it can often be difficult to disentangle them and to find the best place to start.

If this is not taken into account early on, then it can sometimes lead to a disappointing stalemate and a lack of focus in therapy. An example of this is someone who has suffered with both depression *and* anxiety for many years. One form of psychological therapy that is very effective for anxiety is graded exposure therapy. This is sometimes referred to as systematic desensitisation. In this type of therapy the person is first taught some relaxation techniques. They are then encouraged to identify a situation that makes them anxious and that they have tended to avoid. The idea is that they gradually spend more time in the feared situation until they become accustomed to it without being overwhelmed by anxiety. In the most straightforward form of this kind of therapy, the person is also encouraged to keep a diary of their thoughts and feelings and to do 'homework tasks' between sessions. Usually, these tasks involve gradually staying in the anxiety-provoking situation a little longer each time whilst practising the relaxation techniques they have learnt. Of course, this is emotionally demanding work in its own right because it involves steadily confronting one's fears, but the results are often well worth the effort. However, if that same person is also suffering from depression, then they are less likely to feel motivated to take on the challenge than someone who is not depressed. If they have a setback in therapy, they are also more likely than others to take a negative view of their progress and to assume either that it was all 'a waste of time' or that they have 'failed again'. Of course, these assumptions are only likely to make the depression worse. At worst, an increase in their depressive feelings could lead them to drop out of therapy before they have reaped the benefits.

Because of the way that one condition can interact with another, it is essential that psychological therapy proceeds on the basis of a thorough assessment. We shall return to this in Part IV when we look at ways that you can help to make sure that you get the most from psychological therapy. As we shall see, one way you can do this is to be as clear as possible about the nature of the difficulties you have been experiencing and to be willing to think about how they might be linked with other problems in your own background.

Childhood sexual abuse can increase the risk of an individual developing any one, or more, of the conditions described above. However, it is also important to remember that there are many other causes for mental health difficulties, and it would be unhelpful to assume that one's experiences of childhood sexual abuse are automatically the sole cause of any problems one might experience as an adult.

In Part II, we saw that childhood sexual abuse is more likely to occur in situations in which the child's home life is disturbed and emotionally turbulent, which also increases the risk of adjustment difficulties and developmental problems. It is often the case that children who have suffered more severe and prolonged sexual abuse also tend to have suffered significant emotional neglect and physical abuse. Again, all of these factors can combine to create a very unhelpful situation in terms of a child's development and overall adjustment. It can be tempting to try to separate these issues out so that we can conclude that a particular event *caused* a particular problem. However, it is often more helpful to consider the child *and* the adult in context and to take a holistic view, lest we be tempted to jump to conclusions that are too simplistic and unrealistic. Perhaps the best way to think about this is to appreciate that experiences of childhood sexual abuse are often one aspect of a childhood that may have been negative and damaging in a number of ways.

An integrated approach

The technical language that professionals use to make diagnoses does not always tell the whole story. For instance, one difficulty is that simply establishing a diagnosis based upon the person's current symptoms tells us very little about *why* that person is suffering from particular symptoms. Interested readers should refer to the recently developed *Psychodynamic Diagnostic Manual* (PDM Task Force 2006) as an example of a framework that attempts to link 'symptoms' more closely with an understanding of subjective experience and personality development. Too keen a focus on symptoms alone may lead to missing the link between the current symptoms and early experiences. If the person were then to be treated for the surface symptoms, without an understanding of the underlying difficulties, the effects of the treatment risk being short-lived. An example might be someone who has visited their GP complaining of symptoms of anxiety on a number of occasions. Anxiety is often treated with medication and this might well ease the symptoms quite quickly. However, when the prescription runs out, the person might be back to square one and at risk of falling into a pattern of more long-term reliance upon medication. By contrast, if it were possible to explore the roots of the anxiety, then a different treatment choice might emerge. For example, we might discover that the person's recent bouts of anxiety were related to their feelings of jealousy and insecurity in their relationship with their partner. If we were to use Attachment Theory to explore this further, we might also discover that this had been a repeating pattern for many years. Further exploration might reveal that the feelings of insecurity stemmed from a range of neglectful early experiences. If, at that point, the person were to try using an appropriate form of psychological therapy in order to continue making links between harmful past experiences and their present-day symptoms, then some of the difficulties may begin to subside for good. So whilst identifying symptoms is a helpful start, looking at one's difficulties and one's life *in the round* can be equally useful. This is a particular strength of taking a more psychological approach.

The problem of secondary gain

Sometimes a person's symptoms and the restrictions these impose on their life can be seen as a way of the person protecting themselves from something they fear will be even worse. For example, someone who has periodic bouts of social anxiety might eventually stop receiving invitations to go out from their friends. If, behind their anxious symptoms, they were also extremely afraid of being abandoned by someone they were dependent upon, then the 'symptoms' of anxiety might actually help to protect them from something that frightens them even more. This effect is sometimes referred to as 'secondary gain' (van Egmund 2003). It is very important to be aware of this trap because it can make all the difference to the outcome of psychological treatment. For example, if you seek therapy for anxiety but are secretly invested in hanging on to the anxiety for fear of living your life in a different way, then the treatment is less likely to work. Taking the time to consider how issues such as secondary gain apply to you takes courage and a willingness to be open about the possibility of their being a 'pay-off' to your symptoms.

Normal reactions to abnormal circumstances

It is especially important at this stage to emphasise a point that can have profound effects in therapy. This involves considering the idea that the long list of symptoms and difficulties explored so far can sometimes be seen as normal reactions to abnormal circumstances. *Anyone* in a situation where they are being exploited, hurt, threatened, coerced and mistreated is likely to react with a mixture of fear, anger, confusion and shame. *Anyone* who has been bullied, manipulated, humiliated and abused is likely to fear it happening again and to react with anger and anxiety at the slightest hint of a repetition. This is simply human nature. We all *learn* quickly when a threat to our well-being is involved; this type of learning is instinctual and is difficult to undo. The vast array of symptoms, problems and difficulties described in Parts II and III are all possible reactions to sexual abuse in childhood. As such, they are normal reactions to very abnormal circumstances. Children are not supposed to be sexually abused – that is why their minds and bodies react so negatively. It is not because there is something *wrong* with them; it is because the act of abuse itself is fundamentally wrong. It is not a sign of weakness to be traumatised by terrible events in your past. It is not a character flaw to be frightened of meeting new people or of forming new relationships if your trust has been betrayed at an early age. It is not a sign of frigidity or selfishness to be wary of sexual relationships as an adult if you were forced into having sex as a child. These are all understandable reactions. They are all normal reactions to abnormal events. The shame and guilt that often accompanies abuse can leave the person feeling as though it was all their fault. As they continue to struggle with the consequences in later life, they can feel too ashamed to look back to even consider the cause. This is a central aspect of sexual abuse, since it often leaves the person feeling wrapped up in their own self-doubt.

It can often mark a major turning point in psychological therapy when someone, who has lived a significant part of their life blaming themselves for what happened, begins to reach this conclusion for themselves. Because sexual abuse is so personally intrusive and so stigmatising, it can be difficult to consider yourself as a normal person to whom abnormal things happened, not because you were bad or deserved to be treated that way, but because someone exploited their power over you. Sexual abuse is not a reflection on the child, it is a reflection on the perpetrator; how sad and unfair then that it so often seems to be the child who is left carrying the shame.

Review and exercise

In Part III we looked at some of the long-term effects that childhood sexual abuse can have on adults. A range of symptoms and conditions were explored, and some of the technical jargon that is used in diagnosis was explained. This should help you feel more confident about using the terms if the need arises.

Post-Traumatic Stress Disorder and Borderline Personality Disorder were then explored in more detail. This is because childhood sexual abuse has been identified as one cause of these conditions, and it is important to understand the possible links.

It was then acknowledged that *everyday life* is often more complicated than thinking about one set of symptoms or another, and that difficulties often overlap.

At this stage, take some time to reflect on what you have read. Then try to answer some of the following questions for yourself:

- How would you describe the things that are causing you the most difficulty at this point in your life?
- If several things are troubling you, how would you prioritise them?
- What role do you feel events in your childhood have had in creating these difficulties for you?
- Which aspects of your childhood do you think had the most impact on you as an adult?
- How would you explain these feelings and ideas to someone new?

Part IV

Psychological therapy

14 Introduction

Making links and making choices

So far in this book we have used our knowledge of child development to help us understand what can happen when your childhood has been affected by sexual abuse. We looked in detail at how sexual abuse can reshape the emotional 'map' of the world that you carry with you into adulthood. We have also seen that the after-effects of childhood sexual abuse are probably as varied as the human fingerprint. There is no 'standard' response. With this as our starting point, we can now begin to move on and think about ways in which things can be changed so that your life can begin to take a different course.

By this point you may have decided that psychological therapy could be of benefit to you. You may also have recognised reflections of yourself in the various descriptions of symptoms and difficulties. Hopefully you now feel more confident to step back and take a second look at how things have turned out for you and are ready to begin to think about the way ahead. What you have read so far may have reminded you of what you may already know deep down; that things could be different, even in some small way. Hopefully this has brought some relief as well as strengthened your motivation.

In order to help signpost the way ahead, it is also important to consider the other side of the coin. This is because taking the idea of *change* forward will have consequences for you and for the other people in your life. Working through your past can be a painful journey. For example, you may begin to feel tremendous resentment towards the people in your past. You might also begin to feel guilty and ashamed that you did not say 'stop', because that is what you may have felt you 'should' have done – no matter how impossible or unrealistic that would have been. So, along with the relief of feeling better may come the difficult feelings of resentment, regret, anger and shame. Because psychological therapy can be an intense process, it is useful to think about how you will look after yourself and the people around you along the way.

Taking a step forward often involves risk and the inevitability of dealing with strong feelings. This can be very liberating. However, if strong feelings have previously led to a sensation of falling apart or feelings of serious instability then, clearly, it is wise to proceed with caution.

The prospect of 'change', your expectations and some of the possible obstacles to change are described in more detail in the next chapter. Try to keep these thoughts in mind as you work through the rest of the chapters. For example, try to imagine how you would respond to each of the different types of psychological therapy as they are described below. Examples of a 'typical' session are included for each approach to help set the scene.

Then take a careful look through the 'ground rules' for therapy. These ground rules set out, in general terms, what to expect from therapy and what is expected of you if you are to get the best from it.

Part IV ends with an overview of some of the other issues that can arise over the course of therapy. Of course, issues such as shame can be especially important to consider if you have experienced childhood sexual abuse and this can be a big obstacle to overcome. But it is also well worth taking the time to think about the 'practicalities' of going into therapy. Making time for it and ensuring it is not rushed or treated as an afterthought will all help you to get the most from it.

By considering these things ahead of time you will be helping yourself to make the right choice for you. The first step is to establish some realistic priorities.

Establishing a focus

Having a focus is an important starting point in therapy. Of course, it can change over time, but having an idea of what the main problems are for you will help to set the scene. So, where is it best to start? One way to sort this out is to try answering some questions.

- Make a list of some of the problems you feel you have right now.
- From this list, how many of the problems are to do with practical or physical difficulties? For example, are they mainly related to major financial worries, housing problems, aches and pains or some other kind of physical illness?

- How many of the problems would you describe as being emotional? For example, do you struggle with difficulties in relationships? Do you have problems with anger, anxiety or depression?
- Of the emotional problems you have listed, which is causing you the greatest distress right now?
- Similarly, which problem would make the biggest difference to your life if you were able to resolve it right now?

When you have answered these, try to answer the following questions:

- What do you think the realistic 'focus' of any psychological therapy should be right now?
- How would you describe it to someone else who did not know you?

Lastly:

- Given the difficulties you have described above, how would you know that therapy had been successful?

The last question is based upon the idea of the 'miracle question'. The miracle question is a technique that is often used in Solution Focused Therapy (De Shazer 1985), but many types of therapist use it as a starting point. The client is asked to imagine that a miracle has happened and that the problems that had brought them to therapy had all been resolved. Then, the client is asked to describe, in as much detail as possible, how they would really like their life to be. Of course, it is something that you can keep on coming back to again and again, adding in increasing amounts of detail each time. The ideas that come out of the exercise can be used to provide some clear goals for both therapist and client to work towards. Try using the 'miracle question' now to help clarify what you need to work towards changing.

If your current problems are largely practical or physical, then it may well be best to try to sort these out first. Having these things settled will help you to make the most of psychological therapy later on by providing you with a sense of stability in your everyday life. Otherwise, you may find that you are so preoccupied with other problems that it is hard to focus on yourself and how you can change as a person.

Given that you have some goals in mind, do some of your difficulties seem much more pronounced and immediate than others? For instance, if you are struggling to deal with drug and alcohol misuse, or if your symptoms have been particularly severe in the past, it is important to think about achieving as much *stability* as you can before going into therapy. Some of these issues are considered in more detail below.

Drugs and alcohol

In general, the *more* a person is relying on drugs and alcohol, the *less* they are likely to gain from therapy, especially if the focus is on resolving past painful experiences. Often people use substances in order to avoid their feelings. So, if you are someone who has continued to use drugs and alcohol in this way to fend off your feelings, then you are only likely to experience therapy as unsettling. At worst, it may trigger you to rely even more heavily on substances for relief.

Alcohol and other drugs will restrict your ability for thinking and feeling in a meaningful way in therapy. As a general rule, and if you want to give yourself the best chance of gaining something substantial from therapy, tackle your drug and alcohol use first. This might mean seeking specialist support from a dedicated substance misuse service. Another guideline is to stay 'clean' for at least six months before trying to access psychological therapy for other issues apart from your substance misuse.

For background information, the current UK guidelines for safe drinking are:

- Men should drink no more than 21 units of alcohol per week (and no more than four units in any one day).
- Women should drink no more than 14 units of alcohol per week (and no more than three units in any one day).

One unit of alcohol is 10 ml, by volume, of pure alcohol. So, one unit of alcohol is roughly the same as:

- Half a pint of ordinary strength beer, lager or cider (3–4 per cent alcohol by volume), or
- A small pub measure (25 ml) of spirits (40 per cent alcohol by volume), or
- A standard pub measure (50 ml) of fortified wine such as sherry or port (20 per cent alcohol by volume).

Similarly, there are one and a half units of alcohol in:

- A small glass (125 ml) of ordinary strength wine (12 per cent alcohol by volume).
- A standard pub measure (35 ml) of spirits (40 per cent alcohol by volume).

Further information on safe limits for alcohol use can be found by following the links in the Further Information, Links and Contacts section at the back of this book. However, if you are regularly drinking more than the amounts above, then you risk wasting your time and effort by entering therapy unless it is explicitly targeted at helping you to reduce your alcohol use.

More severe symptoms

As discussed in Parts II and III, the range of symptoms and conditions associated with childhood sexual abuse is very broad. However, the more severe any of these conditions have been for you, the more caution should be exercised when seeking psychological therapy. For instance, if you have been treated for a major psychiatric illness or have been hospitalised when your symptoms have been at their height, it is most important to consider how psychological therapy will form part of a *combined treatment approach*. In practice, this may mean that a psychiatrist, a general practitioner (GP) and a psychological therapist will work together to provide a combined treatment package. For instance, medication might be the first stage. Following a given period of stability (ideally of some months), therapy might be considered as the next step, but with a safety net in place in the form of regular reviews with the psychiatrist or GP. This will help to ensure that any risk of relapse is prevented as much as possible, whilst giving you the opportunity to make the best of therapy.

Similarly, if you suffer from a condition such as severe depression, one problem is that you may well feel exhausted just battling with the symptoms. This means you are less likely to have the energy to see friends or to make plans for the future, let alone have the motivation to engage in therapy. If you have reached this point, then it may be that medication will be useful to lift your mood and give you some relief from the negativity so that you can begin to make some other changes. If you are in any doubt, it may be very useful to seek professional advice from your GP and, if necessary, a psychiatrist.

Having considered these issues, you can start to think in more detail about the kind of therapy that is most likely to help you.

Are you looking for support or help to change?

If we sketch out a map of the different kinds of therapy, we can place 'supportive' therapy on one side and 'change'-focused therapy on the other. The focus in supportive therapy is often on keeping things going and achieving more stability in your life rather than making big changes. By contrast, other types of therapy focus on establishing the problem areas and then encourage you to try out new ways of doing things.

Counselling can be seen as more towards the supportive end of the scale. For instance, a counsellor will listen to you carefully and then comment on what you have said in a non-judgemental, empathic and supportive way. A counsellor working in this way is less likely to give you direct advice or explicit guidance. Instead, they will quietly wait for different themes and issues to emerge and then comment on them and invite you to think about what they have said. Counsellors are unlikely to *drive* the process along as much as in other forms of therapy. Many people benefit from having the opportunity just to speak to someone who is ready to hear what they have to say and to help them look at these issues. However, because the sessions can sometimes feel unstructured, it does not suit some people, especially if they are frightened by having a 'blank canvas' to work with.

In the middle of the map we can place the more active approaches of short-term Psychodynamic Psychotherapy, Cognitive Behavioural Therapy (CBT) and Eye Movement Desensitisation and Reprocessing (EMDR). In all of these approaches there is more emphasis on actively setting the goals together. You then work collaboratively with your therapist to focus on particular issues and themes as a means of achieving those goals.

At the far end of the map we might find the more exploratory long-term approach of more traditional psychoanalysis. This kind of treatment is characterised by the quiet attention of the analyst on your words, and by comments or interpretations designed to highlight and bring forward unconscious feelings and material. It is possible to achieve deep levels of change with this kind of approach, but it requires a more long-term commitment.

Of course, it is important to emphasise that all of these approaches rely on the basic ingredients of good therapy, such as a good 'working alliance' (Greenson 1965) or rapport between client and therapist. Research indicates that the stronger the rapport, the more likely it is that therapy will be successful (Horvath and Symonds 1991). From the client's perspective, the quality of the rapport will partly depend on how comfortable they feel with the techniques their therapist uses. For example, some people will find the relative silence of a psycho-analytic psychotherapist overwhelming. By contrast, other people really value the open space this gives them to explore whatever comes to mind.

In the next chapter, some specific types of psychological therapy are described in more detail. Once again, as you read through, try to consider how you would react to each of the approaches described. Thinking about these kinds of issues in advance will help you to choose the right kind of therapy for yourself early on.

15 Psychological therapies

Counselling

Counselling can take many forms (such as Person-Centred, Existential and Humanistic) but, at its heart, it is based upon the 'core conditions' of genuineness, empathy and a non-judgemental attitude (Rogers 1951). In practice, this means that a counsellor will strive to provide you with a relationship in which you do much of the talking. The counsellor, in turn, will listen and comment on what you have said. Often this may be just to encourage you to say more, or to ask you to reflect on your feelings at any given point. It is the counsellor's careful, empathic attention that will help you to reflect on your own words and talk about your feelings as they emerge.

Because counsellors may also be trained in a number of additional models, they may adapt their technique in line with how they sense that you are progressing. For instance, it is not unusual for an experienced counsellor to help you to use some Cognitive Behavioural Therapy (CBT) techniques to help manage your anxiety before exploring other issues in more depth. Once they have helped you with that, they may use a more Psychodynamic approach (see below) in order to gently encourage you to make more links between past and present.

In general, counselling tends to be short term. In the NHS, contracts of six to twelve sessions are fairly typical. Of course, if you pay for counselling privately, the contract could be open-ended and you would decide together when to bring the sessions to an end.

What is a typical session like?

Counselling sessions are usually 50 minutes long. Your counsellor will usually collect you from the waiting area and show you to the counselling room. This could be in a clinic or perhaps in the GP surgery. Ideally, the room will be quiet, warm and free from interruptions. There will be two comfortable chairs, facing each other but at a slight angle.

In a first session, having introduced themselves, your counsellor may begin by telling you a bit about their approach and about how they work. They will also tell you how long the sessions will be and how often you will meet. Then, they will usually ask what brings you to counselling. This is your chance to try to put into words what has been troubling you. Take your time and try not to worry about whether you are making sense or getting everything in order. Many people worry that they are 'rambling', but talking freely is an important part of the work. Your counsellor will listen carefully and when you reach a natural pause they will check back with you what they heard. This process of reflection can be very useful. For instance, hearing that someone else has understood you can be a powerful experience that brings some immediate relief. It can also be very helpful to hear how the counsellor sometimes uses different words to describe what you have said. Putting a different light on things in this way can often help you to think about your difficulties from a new perspective.

Because it is a flexible approach, counselling can be tremendously supportive, but it can also help you to begin to make important changes and to rethink the way ahead.

Many people make good progress in counselling and they use the experience to help them approach things in a different way well after the sessions have come to an end. For some people, counselling can help them to identify some of the more deep-seated problems that will not be resolved in a short number of sessions. In such cases, it also provides a good opportunity to talk with a professional about the prospect of longer-term therapy at some point in the future, as in the case example below:

Case example – Sarah

Sarah eventually settled down with a partner and they had two children together, a girl and then a boy, two years apart. The relationship with her partner was basically okay, but their sex life virtually disappeared once they had children. This led to arguments, which never seemed to get resolved. Sarah noticed that she favoured her son over her daughter. In fact, she could be cold and critical towards her daughter and did not feel much empathy for her, even when she was upset. When her daughter reached school age, Sarah thought she would feel some relief; instead, she felt panicky and overprotective and repeatedly quizzed her daughter about events at school. It was as if she was looking for evidence that something awful had happened to her during the day. This drove even more of a wedge between them and Sarah began to feel that she was at her wit's end.

Sarah went to her GP complaining of feeling anxious and tired all the time. The GP offered some mild medication to take the edge off the anxiety and asked Sarah to come back for a follow-up. On the next visit the GP referred Sarah to the counsellor. When the appointment came through, Sarah panicked and did not attend. She phoned the day after to say she had not been able to make it and asked to be offered another appointment. This time she went along.

The first session was not easy and Sarah struggled to know where to start. The counsellor listened patiently and just asked Sarah to describe what she was feeling and what had been on her mind. By the third or fourth session, Sarah was able to talk about some of the things that had troubled her as she was growing up. The counsellor asked if Sarah thought that her own experiences were now affecting her relationship with her daughter, who was around the same age as Sarah had been when the abuse started. Sarah began to cry, but knew that she had begun to understand something very important to her.

Sarah did well in counselling. After twelve sessions she felt that she had a lot to think about for the time being. She felt less panicky and believed that she understood herself a little better. She tried harder with her daughter, both to be with her when she could, but also to give her space to be her own person too. In the last few sessions Sarah talked with her counsellor about the idea of longer term therapy. Sarah's counsellor agreed that it might be helpful and suggested that Sarah should see how things go for a while, whilst thinking about asking for longer term therapy in the future if things got difficult again.

As with Sarah in the example above, counselling can be a good introduction for longer term therapy because there are many similarities. If you have had a period of counselling and it worked for you, then you will probably find it easier to make use of longer term therapy in the future. You will be familiar with the process and you can also draw on your previous experiences to help you set new goals.

Cognitive Behavioural Therapy (CBT)

Cognitive Behavioural Therapy, or CBT, is built upon a number of basic principles developed by Aaron Beck (1970) and others in the

1960s and 1970s. CBT has its roots in Behaviour Therapy (Skinner 1953), which emphasised the role of learning in shaping human behaviour. But CBT has very effectively combined this body of knowledge with Cognitive Therapy (Ellis 1962; Meichenbaum 1975; Beck 1976). Cognitive Therapy is based on the idea that how we *think* about any given situation will determine how we experience it. This will determine how we *feel* about it and influence our behaviour in that situation. For example, someone who had been trapped in a lift may *learn* that lifts do, indeed, break down and that the experience can be unsettling. If the experience had really upset them, then we can easily imagine, the next time they are in the same situation, that they might feel anxious at the sight of the lift doors opening and decide to take the stairs. This is an example of how experiences influence learning and how learning affects how we perceive similar situations in the future. If our perception is that we are in danger, then we are more likely to change our behaviour accordingly. This was discussed in some detail earlier in relation to Post-Traumatic Stress Disorder (PTSD).

At the heart of CBT is an implicit understanding of the role that our thoughts about events play in determining our emotional reactions, our physical responses and our behaviour. This is represented below:

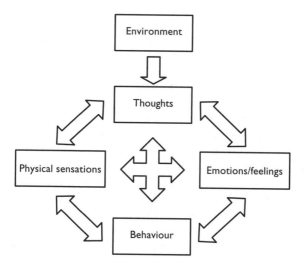

Figure 15.1

This model, known as the 'hot cross bun' model (Padesky and Greenberger 1995), is an elegant way of representing how these different areas link up and affect each other. Thoughts, emotions, physical sensations and behaviour constantly interact with each other *and* with the environment around you. This can include all kinds of influences, including social and cultural factors, the effect of your family upon you as an individual and other aspects of your environment, including housing and finances. Clearly, these factors can have both positive and negative effects upon you at any one point in your life.

CBT works by allowing you to explore – and then change – the links between your thoughts, emotions, physical reactions and behaviour. It is also important to acknowledge that positive changes in one area can have positive effects in the others. Because of this, therapy can be adapted to where *you* are most comfortable starting. For example, some people begin therapy by learning how to physically relax before moving on to look at their thinking style in more depth. By contrast, others might begin by exploring their thinking patterns in relation to particular situations that they find difficult. CBT is a powerful and adaptable approach that is used to treat a very wide range of symptoms and conditions (Hawton *et al.* 1996; Tarrier *et al.* 1998).

What is a typical session like?

Like other forms of talking therapy, CBT usually involves weekly 50-minute sessions. CBT involves using ideas such as the hot cross bun model in order to build up a detailed *map* of how you, as an individual, respond to certain situations or 'triggers'. Cognitive Behavioural Therapists also use a range of techniques in addition to talking your difficulties through with you. For example, they might ask you to challenge some of the 'automatic thoughts' and assumptions that occur in difficult situations by testing them out using behavioural 'experiments'. The nature of the experiments will vary according to the situations you identify as being difficult. Examples include going into a crowded place or attending a meeting you would otherwise avoid. You might be asked to monitor your experiences as you work through some behavioural experiments by keeping a diary of your thoughts, feelings and behaviours. You can use your diary entries in the next session in order to identify particular ways of thinking. Examples include 'expecting the worst' or catastrophising. For instance, someone who is anxious about going in to crowded places may catastrophise this by telling themselves that they will faint or have a panic attack. Once you have spotted how *you* tend to think about things, you will then be encouraged to challenge these ideas. Then you will be given help to try out more flexible ways of looking at the world to see if they can help you to improve your quality of life.

At a deeper level, CBT can also help you to explore and challenge your 'schema' (Salkovskis 1996; Young *et al.* 2003). Schemas, as described in chapter 7, are patterns of deeply held beliefs that we have about ourselves that can have a profound and enduring influence on the way we think, feel and behave. Schemas have their roots in childhood and adolescence, and can be significantly influenced by negative experiences in childhood. For instance, childhood sexual abuse can lead to the development of particular schemas around 'mistrust'. One belief, inherent in this kind of schema, may be that 'other people can never be trusted'. In close relationships this kind of schema might give rise to a fear of dependency and of showing vulnerability to others. These uncomfortable feelings might trigger the impulse to push other people away before they get too close. CBT at this level is sometimes referred to as Schema Therapy. The aim of therapy is to identify problematic – or maladaptive – schema and to challenge them based on the present rather than the past. Making the links between thoughts, feelings and behaviours at this level within a supportive relationship with your therapist can be a powerful therapeutic experience.

Case example – Mark

A friend encouraged Mark to see a counsellor about his drug use. After a couple of false starts, he eventually went along and managed to cut down his alcohol and cannabis misuse. The problem was he then became increasingly agitated and irritable. He had begun to think back over his past and he found himself replaying disturbing scenes from his childhood over and over again in his head. Mark appeared quite depressed and he was finding it difficult to move on with his life.

Mark mentioned this to his GP, who suggested he be referred for CBT to help with his depression. The therapist began by assessing Mark's difficulties and concluded that he was suffering from depression and from low self-esteem. They moved on to explore some of Mark's thoughts about himself and, to help the process along, he was asked to fill in a 'mood diary' when he noticed his mood dipping or when things upset him during the week. He was asked to note down the details of the situation, to describe what was going through his mind at the time and how this had affected his mood.

Mark's therapist asked him to give an example from his diary for them to work with. Mark said he had been out with a friend who had taken a call on his mobile. The friend apologised to Mark, but said he had to leave, his girlfriend was expecting him and he had to go. Mark noticed that this made him feel annoyed, but also quite flat and depressed. He described thinking 'what's the point? No one really wants to know me anyway. . .'. Mark's therapist used a CBT technique called the 'downward arrow technique' and asked him, if it was true that no-one liked him, what would that mean about him as a person? Mark said that it would mean 'no-one would ever like him'. Together they carried on using the technique until Mark arrived at a statement that surprised him: he said that behind it all he believed he was unlovable and that sooner or later people would find out that there was something damaged about him. Mark became upset at this point. He realised that he had said out loud something that he had believed about himself, deep down, for a very long time. Together with his therapist, he explored how this basic assumption about himself had affected many areas of his life. This helped him to understand why he kept people at arm's length and why he felt so hurt when they seemed to push him away.

As in this example, CBT is very much a collaborative therapy. You work together with your therapist to explore your own thoughts, feelings and behaviour. It is a very active therapy and, like all forms of psychological treatment, requires strong motivation and the commitment to keep going, even when things get tough.

Psychodynamic and Psychoanalytic Psychotherapy

Psychoanalytic Psychotherapy is based upon the theory and practice of Psychoanalysis, pioneered by Sigmund Freud (1894). Over the last 100 years, Freud's theories, and their practice, have undergone plenty of revision and development. The practice of psychotherapy is now a 'broad church' from short-term Psychodynamic Psychotherapy (Malan 1979) right through to Psychoanalysis (Sandler *et al.* 1992; Bateman and Holmes 1995), with a wide range in-between. Differences in approach are often a reflection of differences in training and in the background of the therapist. All of these approaches fit under the umbrella of 'Psychotherapy' and there are many overlaps between them. However, there are also important differences to consider in terms of the number and frequency of sessions. For example, short-term Psychodynamic Psychotherapy usually uses weekly sessions for a period of 20 sessions or so. This is the form of psychotherapy you are most likely to find in the NHS. By contrast, Psychoanalytic Psychotherapy is usually practised at the rate of two or three sessions per week and the contract is often open-ended. Further along the scale, Psychoanalysis can be as often as five times per week. Once again, Psychoanalysis can be open-ended, and it is not unusual for the therapy to go on for several years. In many ways Psychoanalytic Psychotherapy can be seen as representing the middle ground.

A basic principle of psychotherapy is the idea that we are all motivated to avoid emotional pain and uncomfortable feelings in one way or another. As a result, we tend to get anxious about certain feelings in case they will be overwhelming or 'unacceptable' in some way. In order to avoid feeling anxious, we try to suppress and avoid them. We do this by using a range of 'defence mechanisms'. Familiar examples are denial, repression and projection (Brown and Pedder 1991, 24–31). These are all ways of shutting feelings off inside ourselves or else trying to get rid of them in one way or another. This might include seeing something in someone else that, really, you do not like about yourself and criticising *them* for it rather than confronting yourself. Whilst we can be very aware of some of our own defence mechanisms, the stronger forms are believed to be 'unconscious' or outside of our everyday awareness. The more powerful the defence mechanism, the greater the *cost* will be in terms of our general well-being and self-acceptance. For example, anyone who has suffered from depression will know that it can be an exhausting condition. A Psychoanalytic Psychotherapist would suggest that, in such cases, strong feelings such as anger and loss are being pushed out of awareness in order to protect the individual from what they fear will be further pain. This requires emotional and psychological *effort* in its own right, whether we are aware of it or not. This contributes to the familiar characteristics of depression, such as lethargy and low mood.

Our use of different defence mechanisms changes and develops with age and maturity (Mahler *et al.* 1975). Poor parenting and overwhelming or disturbing events in childhood can affect this process of development, leaving the individual less well equipped for adult life. At times of stress, in adult life, our defences can be challenged. For some people, if their defences are not sufficiently flexible, events in adult life can seem as threatening and as overwhelming as they had been in childhood.

Of course, we all use the mental 'map' that we build up of ourselves and of the world throughout the course of our lives to make sense of what is going on around us as adults. In psychotherapy, this map is 'transferred' onto the relationship with the therapist, where it can be explored, understood and developed – based on the new experience of the therapeutic relationship. As client and therapist work *together* to understand the feelings and conflicts that arise over the course of therapy, old memories and experiences can be explored. Gradually the past begins to lose its hold over the present. In this way, the client has an opportunity, through the relationship with the therapist, to separate past from present and to see how old experiences might be continuing to colour their view of the present.

The evidence base for the different types of psychotherapy described above is very well established (Roth and Fonagy 1996). Many studies have compared Psychoanalytic and Psychodynamic Psychotherapy with other forms of psychological treatment. Psychotherapy has been shown to be a highly effective form of psychological therapy that is practised all over the world.

What is a typical session like?

As with counselling, the emphasis in psychotherapy is for you to do most of the talking. The basic set-up is the same, with two chairs, a quiet room and 50-minute sessions.

This time let's imagine a session midway through treatment. The therapist may begin by simply asking you how things have been since the last session. If you had particular things on your mind since that time, you might start there. Alternatively, you could pick up a theme that had perhaps been building up over the previous sessions.

For instance, you might have been talking a lot about 'trust', having decided at the start of the therapy that this was an important issue for you. You may have explained that, because of your past experiences, you found it very difficult to trust people. By this point, you may also have recognised that this was one reason you had been finding it difficult to get on with your partner. The therapist might ask you other questions about this in order to help you explore the links between past and present in more detail. However, they might also ask how you are feeling in the session and whether you were struggling to trust them as your therapist. This can sometimes feel quite challenging, but it is an invitation to talk about your feelings as they are happening in the room. If you replied that you often found it difficult to be so 'direct' with people, your therapist would take the opportunity to explore some of your fears in more detail. For instance, if you had been physically abused as a child, or heavily chastised for challenging your parents, you might still be frightened of speaking your mind with adults for fear of the consequences. This would be a good example of how the past was being 'projected' onto the present. The honesty and openness within a psychotherapy session would provide you with a safe place to talk these things through without fear.

Case example – Sarah

Sarah's mood began to dip and she became increasingly depressed. This was around the time her daughter had reached adolescence and had begun dating boys. Her son also spent a lot of time with his friends and Sarah's partner had steadily become more distant from her. Sarah began to worry about her future and her mother had also become quite ill. Sarah had benefited from a short course of counselling some years ago, but this time her GP referred her for psychotherapy. He was worried that Sarah's mood was not lifting, despite a trial of anti-depressant medication, and he was aware that she had been helped by therapy in the past.

Sarah was offered six months of weekly sessions with a psychotherapist. In the sessions she was encouraged to discuss her relationships in more detail and to link her pattern of pushing others away to the events around her parents' separation and the sexual abuse that followed soon after. Sarah realised that the trust she had in others as a child had been shattered and that she had never really felt 'safe' once her parents separated. She also recognised that the trust she automatically put in the neighbour (her babysitter) had been very badly betrayed.

Sarah was surprised at the amount of anger she felt towards her mother, whom she felt should have been there and should have protected her. She also realised how overwhelming it had been for her as a child to hold on to two conflicting sets of feelings, being worried about her mum and wanting to help her, but also being angry because she was not around to protect her. At times she thought her mum must have known what was going on but did not care. Now, with her mother becoming increasingly ill, these mixed feelings were surfacing again. Sarah also realised how angry she was towards her father for leaving them so early on. She began to see that, deep down, she had always believed that it was her fault that her parents had separated. She recognised that her relationship with her partner had become very distant partly because she was so frightened of feeling dependent again.

It was a difficult process of discovery, but Sarah used her sessions to begin to understand that she had spent many years pushing people away and keeping them at arm's length because she was so scared of feeling mixed up and trapped once again. Sarah's psychotherapist had helped her to confront this by noticing how she tended to hold back her feelings in the session, as if she did not really want to share them with her psychotherapist. Sarah thought about this a great deal over the week. She started the next session by agreeing that she held her feelings back, but declared that was because she had lost faith that anyone could be *trusted not to take advantage of her when she felt so vulnerable – after all it had happened before.*

Just as in this example, the emphasis in psychotherapy is on exploring the *relationship issues* that emerge over the course of the treatment. For this reason psychotherapy is especially useful for addressing relationship difficulties such as trust, dependency, shame and vulnerability.

Eye Movement Desensitisation and Reprocessing (EMDR)

Eye Movement Desensitisation and Reprocessing, or EMDR, is a treatment procedure that was originated by Dr Francine Shapiro in the 1980s. The procedure has mainly been used in the treatment of PTSD and is especially useful in the treatment of past trauma. However, it has also been used to treat other symptoms and conditions, including anxiety and panic disorders.

EMDR is unique in its use of 'bilateral stimulation'. In practice, the client is asked to visualise an image from memory that vividly represents the original trauma. They are asked to keep the image in mind while they move their eyes from side to side so as to follow the therapist's hand movements. Some therapists use a light moving backward and forward across a special light bar, but the principle of maintaining the eye movements is the same. Proponents of EMDR claim that these eye movements reproduce the same natural eye movement process that occurs in the 'rapid eye movement' – or REM – phase of sleep and that this can accelerate the therapeutic process.

As with other forms of treatment in mainstream use, there is a strong evidence base for EMDR. It is always used within the context of a sound therapeutic relationship and depends, as much as any other approach, on a good rapport between the client and the therapist. Therapists from many different backgrounds use it as part of their practice, including Counsellors, Cognitive Behavioural Therapists and Psychodynamic/Psychoanalytic Psychotherapists.

The goal of therapy is to allow the client to revisit traumatic memories within a *safe* therapeutic relationship. The client is then encouraged to notice how they react physically and emotionally to the traumatic image, and to notice the negative thoughts they have about themselves that may accompany it. Gradually, the client is encouraged to challenge these negative beliefs and to develop more helpful 'self-statements' to replace early beliefs and assumptions.

What is a typical session like?

EMDR sessions can each be up to 90 minutes long. The sessions centre on the use of the eye movement technique and the exploration of traumatic memories. First, your therapist will explain the technique to you in detail and make sure that you are comfortable with the process. You will then be asked to imagine a 'safe place', which should be an image of a special place or situation that helps you feel calm and secure.

Then you will be asked to imagine a scene that reflects the traumatic experience you want to work through. Your therapist will ask you to put some negative words to the image that represent how you actually felt at the time. Examples include 'I am powerless' or 'I am going to die'. Your therapist will ask you to hold those words in mind as you focus on the image. Your therapist will then ask you to follow their hand as they move it backwards and forwards, or they may ask you to track a light moving across a 'light bar'. Every now and again, your therapist will ask you to just *notice* what feelings are coming up as you continue to repeat the eye movements for a minute or so. In between the sets of eye movements, your therapist will talk to you, in detail, about how you feel and what you notice. For instance, some people recall vivid physical sensations, such as a tightness in their chest or a racing heartbeat, as they work through the traumatic memories.

Over time, your therapist will systematically go over your traumatic memories with you. As they do so, they will gradually encourage you to combine the traumatic image with more positive and realistic beliefs that reflect how you feel about those old memories in the here-and-now. Examples include 'I have choices now, I am not powerless now' or 'It's over, I am safe, I'm not going to die'.

You can stop the process at any time and return to your 'safe place' using a pre-arranged signal, such as raising your hand. This means that you are always in control of the process, if you feel that you need some time out.

Your therapist will always end the session by helping you to settle back into a calm and comfortable mood. Typically they will ask you to use your 'safe place' memory to help you reinforce the sense of feeling okay as you prepare to end the session.

Whilst EMDR is a relatively 'new' form of treatment, it is already a well-established treatment approach in its own right (Shapiro 1995; Chemtob *et al.* 2000). EMDR has also been recommended in the evidence-based clinical practice guidelines for the treatment of PTSD by the Department of Health (2001) in the UK and by the National Institute of Clinical Excellence (2005).

Case example – Anna

Anna did not have children and, in her forties, she became increasingly depressed. Her GP had prescribed several different anti-depressants but they seemed to make little difference. Anna was invited to see the counsellor at the surgery. She found it difficult just to 'talk', but her counsellor reassured her that many people felt this way and encouraged her to keep going if she could. Despite this, Anna only went back once more. She was able to say that she found the silences and the counsellor's style difficult; it made her feel so anxious that she found herself not being able to speak. She wondered if there was anything else she could try. Her counsellor referred her to be seen by a Cognitive Behavioural Therapist.

The therapist began by picking up the work that the counsellor had started and by helping Anna to practise some strategies to manage her anxiety a little more. Anna discussed being very anxious from an early age and, in time, she was able to recall, and talk through, how she had felt each night when her stepfather came home. The therapist then discussed some of the characteristic symptoms of Post-Traumatic Stress Disorder with her. Anna felt some immediate relief at this, because it began to explain much of what she had experienced. Her jumpiness, her recoiling from the smell of alcohol and tobacco smoke, her awkwardness around people who had been drinking and her desire to always get home to the safety of being behind a locked door – they all fitted the picture.

Anna's therapist discussed EMDR with her. In the next few sessions they used this method to focus on Anna's memories of her abuse by her stepfather. Anna remembered very vividly the terrible feeling in her chest, as she believed she was going to die of suffocation. Her therapist encouraged her to describe this in as much detail as she could and then to try to let it go as if she was just watching some scenery going by. After several sessions Anna was slowly able to reassure herself that these awful memories belonged in the past and that she was safe now and could look after herself.

Despite her relief at feeling less haunted by her memories, Anna found it extremely upsetting to think back over the 'lost' years, and realised that her life had been shaped by those unwanted childhood experiences. Nevertheless, she was able to see that she had reacted just as anyone else would have done because the situation was so frightening, overwhelming and abusive. Anna's sense of self-blame and shame about what happened slowly began to shift as she continued to talk through what had happened and to break down the traumatic memories.

As the sessions wound down, Anna began to take a few more risks and managed to stop relying on avoidance to get her through. She invited a couple of workmates out for lunch and began to take part in life a little more. For the first time in her life, she booked a holiday abroad and really allowed herself to move beyond the safety and the 'prison' of the life she had made for herself.

Anna was able to make good use of this approach. She was comfortable with the way her therapist described the process to her and the idea that she could move on from old memories appealed to her. EMDR can bring up a lot of issues connected with past traumatic memories. It is an intensive form of treatment, but it can be very effective in moving people beyond their traumatic pasts.

As with any other form of therapy, it is most important that this treatment should only be undertaken with an accredited therapist. This can, of course, be established via the accrediting organisation. One branch of the accrediting organisation is the EMDR Association UK and Ireland. Contact details for this organisation can be found in the Further Information, Links and Contacts section at the end of this book.

Summary

The treatment approaches described above can all be helpful for people who have been sexually abused as children. They all have a strong evidence base and they have well-established organisations behind them dedicated to research, training and accreditation. The Further Information, Links and Contacts section provides more details on these organisations.

Different types of therapist will also provide different types of therapy, depending on their training and further experience. For example, some people will have trained exclusively in CBT or Psycho-analytic Psychotherapy. Other professionals, such as Clinical Psychologists and Counselling Psychologists, have trained in the use of several approaches. People with training and experience in a number of models can integrate different approaches to suit you, drawing techniques from different models accordingly. It is well worth asking about a therapist's training, experience and approach so that you make sure that you find the right type of therapy for you.

There are, of course, many other models and methods that can be useful when treating the after-effects of trauma and childhood sexual abuse. However, as a general rule, it is always important to consider how safe and effective any form of treatment or therapy is, as well as how much you think it will suit you. With the more established and popular approaches, practised by accredited therapists, this is obviously easier to establish. In all cases, it is recommended that you always use the ground rules presented in the next chapter to inform your decision making.

16 Some ground rules for psychological therapy

Before proceeding further with entering psychological therapy, it is important to consider some basic ground rules. This guidance applies to all forms of psychological therapy.

The setting

It is important to remember that a trusting relationship between one person and another is the basis of *any* psychological therapy. Generally speaking, the client and therapist meet regularly for sessions of a set length. This is usually 50 minutes per week. Ideally the appointments should be in the same place and, if possible, at the same time each week. The room should be quiet, comfortable and private. It should be free from unwanted disturbance such as phone-calls, overheard conservations or background noise. The client should understand that the conversation they have with their therapist is confidential. Any *limits* of that confidentiality should also have been discussed and understood.

In a therapeutic relationship the client discusses their difficulties and feelings with the therapist, who is appropriately trained and sufficiently experienced so as to help. Obviously, they should do this with due compassion, concern and professionalism. Because the relationship has particular *boundaries*, the client is freed up from the everyday concerns of handling a friendship or other type of social relationship with their therapist. Of course, client and therapist may have a very strong relationship, but this works precisely because it is different to relationships in the everyday world. For instance, the therapist does not share his or her own problems with the client and does not give casual 'advice' based on their own experience, as one friend might do for another. The framework provided by the therapist's training and approach means that the relationship they offer is *safe*. By talking, the client is able to explore a wide range of difficulties and issues with the help of the therapist, who demonstrates, again and again, that they will listen and seek to understand.

What to expect from your therapist

Professional registration and accreditation

Your therapist should be accredited by a nationally or internationally recognised professional organisation. Please note that this is not, as yet, a statutory requirement in the private sector in the UK. This means that anyone can advertise himself or herself as, for example, a 'Psychologist' or as a 'Psychotherapist'. Registration with a recognised accrediting body therefore ensures that a therapist has fulfilled the requirements of their training committee and holds a current practising certificate. A list of accrediting bodies is provided in the Further Information, Links and Contacts section. There are contact numbers and website addresses, which mean that you can also ask questions about the type of work undertaken by therapists registered with that particular organisation.

You can also search for a 'local' therapist on some organisations' websites and find out how to get in contact with someone near you. A good example of an accrediting body that provides this kind of service is the United Kingdom Council for Psychotherapy (UKCP). Professional bodies such as this have a clear code of ethics that their therapists are obliged to abide by and there is also a formal complaints procedure should anything be amiss. Locating a therapist who is registered with such an organisation therefore helps to guarantee the quality of service you receive and may help to further reassure you as to the safety of the process.

Ethical behaviour

Your therapist should be non-judgemental, non-discriminatory and accepting of you as an individual regardless of ethnicity, religion, sexuality, political persuasion etc. If you feel that this is not the case, then apply the 'speak out' rule (below) and take the opportunity to explore these feelings in more depth. If you are still not comfortable, you may have to reconsider your choice of therapist.

Your therapist should also be punctual and give you advance warning of any changes to your arrangement. They should also be clear about how to contact them outside of session times should that be appropriate and, if you are paying for therapy, they should be clear about the fee structure. For instance, many therapists will charge full fees for a session missed at very short notice, but may also try to reschedule an appointment with sufficient time to do so. However, you cannot take this for granted and, once again, it is important to have these conversations early on.

It is fundamental to any professional training that therapists ensure confidentiality and the proper handling of information. This extends to the sharing of information with others involved in your care (if this is the case). It also means that they should be clear about the limits of confidentiality if, for example, they believe you are at risk in one way or another.

Appropriate boundaries

Boundaries are fundamental to the maintenance of a safe therapeutic relationship. These work both ways and it is your therapist's role to monitor and attend to the boundaries at every point. The provision of appropriate 'boundaries' means that you meet at an agreed time and place. It means that your therapist ensures that sessions do not over-run. It means that your confidentiality is respected and it means that you, as a client, are not exploited in any way. It also means that your therapist maintains a professional relationship with you, which does not stray into a social or sexual relationship, at any point. If you have *any* concerns about the behaviour of a therapist towards you, immediately take it up with them. If you are not satisfied, consider pursuing this with their employer and/or professional body, and talk it through again if possible. If you have been abused in childhood, your sense of appropriate boundaries in relation to others may well have been confused and exploited. When these issues resurface in therapy, it goes without saying that your therapist should be very aware of what is happening and be sufficiently grounded in their own sense of boundaries so that they can help you work this most important issue through.

These are some of the basics of 'good practice'. By way of contrast, a therapist who is vague about their accreditation and qualifications, who is often late, who contacts you on your mobile phone to rearrange sessions at short notice and who insists on *cash* (if you are paying for therapy) warrants serious concern, and is best avoided.

What is expected of you as a client?

Attendance

If you are entering into NHS therapy then, of course, there is no fee. However, it is fundamental that you make every effort to attend the regular sessions offered to you. Many NHS psychological therapy services are under-funded and the time limit imposed on the therapy offered to you may reflect this in some way. There is also often a policy that, after a given number of missed appointments, your case is closed. The reason for this is twofold. Firstly, the service will probably be under pressure to see the next client on the waiting list and the guideline will be that if you are not using the sessions then the time should be offered to the next person waiting for therapy. Secondly, the reasoning may be that if you are not attending sessions regularly then it may be because therapy is too stressful, or else not working, or that it is not the right time. If you are struggling, try to speak out about it and talk it through rather than doing yourself the disservice of missing the opportunity.

It is most important then to consider the realities of engaging in psychological therapy beforehand. It is a serious commitment and, for all sorts of reasons, it may be difficult to manage. Be realistic and do not, for example, set yourself a target of attending sessions first thing across town when you have a hundred and one other things to do each day. Apart from anything else, you are likely to arrive so stressed that you will not be able to use your session to achieve anything other than recover your equilibrium. Make *time* for therapy, before, during and after the session, so that you give yourself the opportunity to really pay attention to what is going on. Try to avoid cramming therapy into your lunch hour. If this is how you operate, ask yourself why you would treat such an important issue in this way – does it reflect something about your characteristic way of treating yourself?

Engaging

It is a golden rule of therapy that you engage with the process as much as you possibly can. The client who is gradually able to allow spontaneity and emotion in the session and who is willing to reflect on the sessions in-between times is likely to gain much more from it. If, after a number of sessions, you do not feel that you can allow more spontaneity or exploration, then it may be time to reconsider your choices. If the attention your therapist offers you just feels intrusive and threatening, then it also may be that this particular form of treatment is not right for you.

However, if you notice that you are beginning to make connections between thoughts and feelings in different situations, and noticing links between your past and your present, then it is likely that therapy is working and that you are engaging well. Of course, it is also likely that the process will be distressing and unsettling at times. However, if on the whole, you are able to hold onto a sense of making some progress, then therapy may well be worth the effort for you.

Realistic expectations

A central aim of this book is to help you engage in therapy by being prepared for what will be asked of you and with realistic expectations. Therapy can help, but only if you are prepared to seek it out, engage with the process and invest some trust in it. If all of these things are in place, then you may well emerge both feeling better *and* functioning better. Key to this is a willingness to be open and honest and to consider your own role in maintaining some of the difficulties you have been experiencing. Remember, change happens in *you*. For example, therapy will not turn your previously disruptive neighbours into different people or instantly boost your employment prospects. However, it may help you to enjoy your life as it is and to begin to make changes that mean you give yourself every chance of happiness.

Speaking out

If there is something you are not happy about in therapy, then mention it. This is often a difficult area, especially if you feel awkward about raising an issue *and* equally awkward about keeping it to yourself. This conflict might also stir up painful feelings associated with abusive relationships in childhood in which 'telling' and 'speaking out' may have felt very threatening or shameful. Overcoming the shame and fear about talking about your feelings is a major goal in therapy and 'working through' those anxieties in the safety of the therapeutic relationship is one of the ways that psychological therapy can be especially helpful.

As a general rule then, it is very important to speak out, even though this might well feel uncomfortable. This is the only way to give yourself the opportunity to explore important issues.

Paying for therapy

Psychological therapy with the NHS is free. It is very likely to be time-limited and there is likely to be a wait before therapy begins. Because of this, and other reasons, you might consider paying for therapy as a way of making treatment more accessible and flexible.

Paying for therapy also creates certain conditions that are important to consider. For example, it means that you are using your money to look after yourself and investing in your mental health and well-being. It is also likely to mean that you attend sessions, even when you do not necessarily feel like doing so, since you are likely to be charged full rate even if you do not attend. It is also likely to raise strong feelings about the past, since you might feel tremendous resentment that you are having to pay to get help to redress the past. Of course, these are important issues that will benefit from being discussed in detail in therapy in their own right.

Considering other options: support groups, survivor networks

There is no *one* right solution to the difficulties we have explored. Many different treatments, therapies and activities can help. You do not have to feel restricted to following any one route, especially if it does not feel right for you. By going another way you have not failed, you are exploring what is right for you and this, in itself, is a most important process. It shows that you are taking care of yourself and listening to your own feelings rather than just to the 'shoulds' and 'oughts' of others, however well-meaning their suggestions.

Similarly, whilst the bulk of this chapter has been about individual psychological therapy, there are many alternatives and parallel paths. For instance, in the UK, there are many support networks that are provided on a voluntary basis, often by others who have suffered similar experiences. They are sometimes referred to as 'survivor' networks. Involvement with a group of others who may have had similar experiences can be a powerful and very supportive experience. However, as with any other form of treatment you might be considering, do some research and look for groups that have a high national profile and that have stood the test of time. As with any other service, consider what you need to know, accept that it may not be right for you and ask if you can meet someone to talk through what joining a group might actually be like. As above, be clear of the ground rules and try to imagine what the experience would really be like for you. Be clear about the commitment and be clear about your expectations – are they realistic? How do these expectations compare with the experiences of someone who has been in the group for some time?

Just making contact with some of these organisations can be a very important step in its own right. It might indicate that you are ready to do something about what has been troubling you. If this is the case, then it is almost certainly going to arouse mixed feelings. One part of you may want to go ahead and do everything that you can to change things, whilst another part of you may feel very anxious, or even guilty, about the idea.

In the next chapter we will look at some other, more general, issues around the idea of going into therapy. At the end of that chapter there is a reminder to stop and review what you have read.

17 More issues to consider before starting therapy

In this chapter there are a number of issues that it would be helpful to think about before going into therapy. They help to set the scene a bit more, but they are also provided as prompts for you to think about how each of them will affect you as an individual.

Mixed feelings

The idea of 'attachment' has already been discussed in some depth, and this can have an impact on your feelings about going into therapy. If your earliest relationships were unpredictable, frightening and abusive, it is understandable that you might find it very difficult to believe that any other relationship could be stable, reliable and safe. Trust and hope can be severely undermined as a result of abuse and neglect. The therapeutic relationship can bring all of these issues into focus.

It is understandable, therefore, and not at all uncommon, to find many people will have very mixed feelings about entering therapy. As a rough guide, approximately 25 per cent of appointments in a typical out-patient psychological therapy service are missed or cancelled at short notice. The reasons for this are many, but it is likely that this is due to anxiety about the reality of taking the first step. Mixed feelings also go with the territory when you are entering the unknown. If you feel that this applies to you, then it may well be a struggle just to attend the first appointment. However, if you can apply the ground rule that is it better to *speak out* about difficult things such as this, then you might find that it helps you and your therapist to be direct about this early on. For instance, if you can begin the session by saying 'I really did not want to come here today. . .', it might feel awkward, but it could well be the best way to start.

Getting in touch with difficult feelings and memories

Being out of touch with your feelings can be one way of dealing with the memories of an abusive past. Staying 'spaced out' or trying to escape your feelings in one way or another is 'protective' because it allows you to keep on going but the cost can be heavy. The long-term effect can be a kind of emotional numbing that means you live your life at one remove.

As you progress through therapy you are likely to find that you feel things more intensely rather than less. This can be a difficult and unexpected experience. But talking about yourself and your past can easily bring strong feelings to the surface, even many years after the event. When this happens, you may be very tempted to turn back and try to push your feelings down again. However, it is always worth being direct about how you feel in therapy – even if this means just explaining that you don't know how to deal with what you are going through.

As therapy progresses further, you may experience many different types of feelings. For example, some people report feeling an intense rage at the person (or people) who abused them and at those whom they feel did not protect them. Because of this, it is very important to give yourself the chance to put these feelings into words in therapy rather than into actions later. If you are in therapy and feeling this way, take it back to your next session, write it down, talk to a highly trusted friend – but always try to avoid taking action until you have given yourself the time to talk the feelings through.

The power of shame

It is important to emphasise the issue of shame because it plays such a central role in the feelings of adults who have been abused as children. Shame can be very inhibiting. It can make entering therapy very difficult and it can make being honest and open with your therapist feel awkward and unsettling.

Once a child realises that what is happening to them, or has happened to them, is wrong, they may suddenly feel that it is all their fault. They may also be very frightened that they will be blamed and judged if anyone finds out. This can obviously lead them to hide behind silence.

This is often the case when a child has been sexually abused. The child might fear shaming themselves and their family by speaking out and so they try desperately to cover up what has happened – at a heavy price. Indeed, the perpetrator may also have reinforced this idea, threatening the child that they will not be believed or that they will be blamed for what happened. From a child's perspective, in a world where adults hold all the power, it is easy to believe what you are being told.

Shame can easily carry over into adulthood. However, with enough time and space in therapy, the fear of being shamed again can be gradually worked through. It is important to share your thoughts and feelings about this in therapy, if you possibly can. Therapy does not mean that you *have* to describe what happened to you in detail; instead, therapy is about understanding *why* that feels such an awful prospect. This means addressing and lifting shame rather than repeating it.

Remembering the past – separating past from present

As therapy progresses, more memories are likely to come to light, both good and bad. Dreams can become more vivid and frequent, everyday experiences may have a more heightened emotional *edge*. If you have suffered from them before, you may also experience more flashbacks for a time. However, as this happens you will also have more opportunity to separate the past from the present by talking it through and exploring its hold over you. The more you are able to do this, the more you can build up the 'self-talk' that reminds you that what happened belongs in the past. Of course, in the early stages, this is something you may find that you need to remind yourself again and again.

Working through the past

As the process of therapy continues, old defences or old ways of looking at the world will break down and give way. This should not feel like a landslide, more like a gradual giving up of old assumptions and beliefs and the trying out of new attitudes and perspectives. However, if therapy feels like you are continually being thrown in at the deep end without a life belt, then it might be moving too fast. If this is the case, then speak out and let your therapist know exactly what is going on for you. A competent therapist would much prefer to hear this than to proceed at a pace that is not helping you. As one piece of 'old' territory gives way you should feel that you have a new piece of the map to step onto. If this is not how it feels, then slow down.

Trust and dependency

These are both likely to be major issues for you, especially if your trust in others was betrayed at an early age. The all-important feelings of hope and enthusiasm towards therapy at the start may soon give way to uncomfortable feelings of a fear of dependency. At that point, part of you may want to withdraw, fearing that getting closer and feeling more dependent will only lead to helplessness and exploitation. Importantly, another part of you may see that there is an opportunity to invest trust in another person and for that to *add* to the quality of the relationship. Once again, a sensitive and competent therapist will be alive to these issues, whichever approach they use. If you bring up your fears and talk about them, then there is much more chance of working them through.

Putting different feelings together

In childhood we make sense of the world by dividing things up into opposites, such as 'good *or* bad' and 'friends *or* enemies'. As adults, we often continue to do this and we might see ourselves, and other people, as 'all good' and 'all bad'. Sometimes we see nothing in between apart from confusion and uncertainty. But when such a cut-and-dried way of dealing with the world is tested in therapy, it can feel very confusing. For example, to trust your therapist *and* to be angry with them at the same time for going on holiday (perhaps just when the work is most important to you) can be very challenging. However, it is also a vital step in dealing with mixed feelings towards other important people in your life.

Being able to hold onto and bear mixed feelings towards the same person – such as love *and* hate, anger *and* care – is a very important step in child development. Therapy can provide an opportunity for these feelings to unfold again and to sit alongside each other more safely. With time, this can generalise into your everyday life. As a result, friendships can become more flexible, relationships can become fuller and your view of yourself can be far less critical and restricted.

Holding on

The courage to hold on even when the going gets tough is central to gaining the most from therapy. The temptation to withdraw and pull away from what we fear is natural. Of course, avoidance makes us feel better *now*, but it only serves to short-change us in the future.

Taking a long-term view, and sticking to something that is not instantly gratifying, can be especially difficult if you felt deprived and neglected in childhood. But holding on and seeing it through might offer a new way of dealing with things. It might mean giving yourself a chance to 'get through' something difficult in order to come out in a better place. Commitment can be tested, especially when the going seems slow or when there are breaks, scheduled or otherwise, in your therapy.

Breaks in therapy

Breaks in therapy, for whatever reason, are likely to be emotional hot spots. This is especially so if your past history has been about broken trust, abandonment and rejection. If you have been treated as 'all good' one moment and as 'all bad' the next, it is also more likely that you will see others in the same way. For instance, the 'good' therapist who takes a break may rapidly fall from grace and seem much more like the 'bad' parent who neglected and ignored you. This can stir up thoughts and feelings that need to be shared and worked through. Strong feelings of resentment at having been *pushed away* may come to the surface, and this can feel unsettling. Once again, try to hold on and apply some of the ground rules above. Speak out about what's on your mind and explore it.

Ending therapy

As with breaks, ending therapy can be difficult. In time-limited therapy, for example within the NHS, there might be little room for manoeuvre in terms of negotiating further therapy straight away. Of course, this can stir up old feelings of having been neglected, which will also benefit from being aired as they occur.

If you are paying for therapy, then ending the work can be something that you negotiate with your therapist for some time in advance. Even if you feel ready to end, and consider that you have achieved as much as you had hoped, working through the ending of therapy is a most important part of the process. The process of letting go, of separating and of moving on can stir up feelings of loss and grief alongside hope for the future. It can also give you a fresh sense of independence and maturity.

An experienced therapist will help you pay particular attention to this period of therapy, even if your inclination is to avoid it and 'make a clean break'. Holding on and staying with that process will allow you to make the most of the work you have done together. Strong feelings can also accompany this step of the journey.

What if you feel worse?

There will probably be times when you feel that therapy is just making things seem worse. But if there is no relief or sense of progress, then it may be that it is just not working for you. There can be many reasons for this (Sandler *et al.* 1992) and it is another reason why it is helpful to have thought your choices through in advance. Signs that things are not improving include an increase in 'acting-out' or dealing with one's feelings through self-destructive or aggressive behaviour. For instance, if you end up falling back upon misusing substances for relief, then therapy has clearly not been helpful. In general, if therapy just feels destabilising and disturbing, then it may be that other sources of help and support should be sought instead.

A certain degree of stability is always required to cope with the changeable tide of the therapy process. This is why a competent therapist will spend time with you at the start in order to conduct an in-depth assessment. One of the main reasons for doing this is to be as sure as possible that therapy will not have a destabilising effect. If previous attempts at therapy have made you feel this way, then this is where you should start with any further therapy. Do not rely on just 'hoping' that it will not happen again. Explore what happened in retrospect and in depth, and make an informed decision as to what is best for you, even if this means opting not to engage in therapy. As a general guide, those people who benefit most from psychological therapy are troubled enough to seek it out, but are also generally stable enough to use it without it causing more problems.

Making changes: the risks and pitfalls

By now, it should be clear that therapy can be a difficult but very rewarding process to engage in. In some ways it will be different for each individual, but making changes, no matter how much it seems like a good idea at the time, means taking risks.

The risks include letting go of your old map of how things are, which can feel disorienting and unsettling. It means taking the risk of doing things differently and approaching some of the things you have tended to avoid. It means taking the risk of allowing yourself to feel vulnerable again and of letting people get close. It also means risking getting your hopes up and risking experiencing strong feelings, which can be both painful and liberating.

Therapists have long recognised that change is a difficult and demanding task and sometimes, despite the best efforts of therapist and client alike, it can seem safer and more reassuring to stay 'stuck'. The concept of 'secondary gain' has sometimes been used to describe this issue (Freud and Breuer 1895). Misapplied, this term can be used in a blaming way to suggest that someone is staying stuck deliberately. However, it is possible to be subtly rewarded by others for staying as we are. For example, someone who is depressed may have been provided with a 'special' place in the family. As a result, there might be less expectation upon them to contribute or to achieve and other people may go out of their way to check that they are okay. If this is the case for you, then 'getting better' is going to mean giving up some of those subtle privileges. It is important to consider, seriously and honestly, this other hidden side of 'getting better'. People do not exist in a vacuum – when they change, other people around them notice this and they can react in different ways. As always, taking the time to really consider how both you *and* those around you might deal with this ahead of time may help later on. Ignoring this side of things means that you may find yourself hitting the same barriers again and again.

Now we will spend some time thinking about what is meant by *change*. Different people mean different things by it, and it is important to have a good sense of what change means to you as an individual.

What is change?

In therapy, change can occur in many different ways and in many different areas. Therapists from different approaches emphasise different areas of change. For example, some focus on improvement in their client's symptoms and see that as the main goal. Others are more likely to consider improvements in the quality of their client's relationships at home as a sign of positive change.

Professionals have traditionally measured change in order to test whether a particular treatment has been successful. Therapists often use psychometric tests in order to take a 'snapshot' of the client's difficulties before and after therapy. It is certainly not unusual to be presented with some form of psychometric test in an assessment session.

In the UK, a much-used example is the Clinical Outcomes in Routine Evaluation (CORE) (Mellor-Clark and Barkham 1998). The

CORE covers four broad areas. These are Subjective Well-being, Symptoms, Life/Social Functioning and Risk/Harm. The CORE has a built-in clinical 'cut-off' and scores above this cut-off suggest that the individual has a clinically significant difficulty in that particular area. Other tests in general use include the General Health Questionnaire (GHQ) (Goldberg 1978), the Hospital Anxiety and Depression Scale (HADS) (Snaith and Zigmond 1983) and the Brief Symptom Inventory (BSI) (Derogatis and Spencer 1982). Some tests focus on particular sets of symptoms, such as depression or anxiety, dissociation or hopelessness. Examples are the Beck Depression Inventory (BDI-II) (Beck *et al.* 1988a) and the Beck Anxiety Inventory (BAI) (Beck *et al.* 1988b). Other examples are the Dissociative Experiences Scale (DES-II) (Carlson and Putnam 1992) and the Impact of Event Scale (IES) (Horowitz *et al.* 1979), both of which are frequently used by trauma treatment services.

Whilst these psychometric measures are important, they are only one part of the bigger picture, which should also take into account both the client's and the therapist's view of how things have changed. These may be much more subtle and personal perspectives are equally valuable if we are to have a balanced and sufficiently rich view of change.

How do you think about change for yourself?

The process of change may not have seemed at all straightforward. It can be more like a gradual widening out of a circle, sometimes with the same events and same periods in your life being revisited again and again – often with more detail and more emotional depth on each occasion.

Change can feel uneven and surprising, and sometimes it feels as if you have actually taken a backward step. However, it can be useful at such times to look back and ask yourself how things were before you entered therapy. For example, how much were you smoking or drinking? How many friends had you avoided and how many opportunities to do something different had you let slip by? You might also ask yourself how you feel right now? For instance, are you less depressed? Is your sex life more satisfying and less awkward or chaotic? Are things at work generally 'okay'? Do you have fewer aches and pains? Do you have more than the occasional 'good' day? All of these are hints at subtle areas of change, and it might only be when you step back that you can see the progress and feel that you really have begun to move away from the past.

This is another reason to keep a journal as you progress through any kind of therapy or therapeutic programme. Not only can this act as an aide-mémoire, it can also encourage you to reflect, in your own time, on particular events in therapy and on what has been stirred up. A journal can also be an important source of reassurance and insight long after therapy has ended. It can be very comforting to look back on changes in your sense of well-being at different points and to see how different stages of the work produced different moods, feelings and thoughts.

A sense of having made progress will fluctuate over the course of time, but it is perhaps reassuring to know that the process of change can often continue well after therapy has ended (Horowitz 1987).

In order to help round up some of these issues, positive change can be thought about as a mixture of the following:

- Improvements in particular symptoms, e.g. less depression and anxiety.
- Feeling more freed up, e.g. less guilt and more spontaneity.
- More hope and optimism.
- More sense of integration, i.e. less need to divide the world into 'all good' and 'all bad'.
- Being more at ease with positive feelings such as love, care and empathy.
- Being more at ease with difficult feelings such as anger, envy, disappointment and loss.
- Improved capacity to *think* and make decisions.
- Improved ability to look after oneself without falling back on self-destructive habits.
- Greater sense of autonomy and individuality.
- Less need to withdraw from reality in times of stress.
- Fewer tendencies to *somatise* or to transform emotional pain into physical pain.

There are, of course, many more dimensions that we could add and the precise pattern of change will be different for each individual. However, in preparing for therapy, it may be especially helpful to start with some of the ideas above and try to decide what the idea of positive change really means for you. Take some time at the end of this chapter to think the idea through and make some notes about the areas that feel most important for you to work on. These might change with time, but they will provide you with a place to start that can also help you stay focused and motivated. Motivation is a major factor determining who does well in therapy, but it can go through different phases and may seem to ebb and flow depending on where you are in therapy and how you are feeling. Having clear goals is one way to shore that up (Michalak and Holtforth 2006).

The practical side of things

Because therapy is demanding and because making changes can be challenging, it is always important to be aware that you may well feel worse before you start to feel better. With this in mind, it is best to consider how this might affect you and how you can have as many protective 'buffers' around you as possible. Some of the things that help people with this are as follows.

Support networks

As above, partners, friends and family can be an important source of support during the process of therapy. It is likely that having well-trusted people around who will understand when you are going through a particularly rough patch will make the going easier. Encouragement from those whose opinion you value can also help you to stay in touch with how far you have come in moving away from your past and really living in your present. By contrast, a partner who is critical of your efforts or who wonders why it is all 'taking so long' is likely to make things feel more difficult.

Timing

It is important to consider this ahead of arranging therapy. For instance, it would be unwise to go into therapy when you are about to move house, when there is some other major upheaval going on in your life or when you have some other major 'practical' issues to attend to. Ignoring these issues is only likely to cause more stress later on.

Good timing means getting a balance between knowing what you want to achieve, knowing how you can go about it and making sure that arrangements are in place that will help you to go ahead.

Of course, it can also be difficult in the midst of a busy life to just put time aside for therapy. One suggestion is to try giving yourself a good half an hour each side of the session where you have no other regular commitments. For example, you might want to spend some time alone before and after a session and, if you drive to your session, you might want to feel that you can gather your thoughts before heading off into traffic again.

Psychological work can be every bit as draining as physical work. It might also be useful to bear this is in mind when planning *when* and *where* to see your therapist. For example, an appointment last thing on a Friday afternoon may be convenient for your employer, but it may mean that you are physically and emotionally washed out before you even arrive at your session. Recognising the importance of the sessions and arranging them for a time when you know you can make them can be an important motivator.

Back-up plan

Finally, having a back-up plan will be useful, even if you never use it. This should include other options apart from therapy, which you may wish to explore if therapy does not turn out to be as rewarding as had been hoped. Other things can also get in the way of therapy, such as ill health or changes in the lives of important people around you. If you have other options available, then stopping therapy or taking a break will feel less threatening. There are many options, but suggestions include taking up a sport, going to the gym or starting out in a relaxation class. Once again, it is worth taking the time to think this through for yourself so that you are prepared.

Review and some final thoughts

This book has covered many issues related to childhood sexual abuse. In reading through – and stopping to reflect on how the material relates to your own life story – you have taken some significant steps. If you decide to go into psychological therapy, this will have helped you to prepare in advance.

We began by considering the widespread problem of childhood sexual abuse. This involved looking at some of the research and taking an overview of the impact that childhood sexual abuse can have.

Then we looked at the process of child development in more detail. By appreciating the tremendous tasks involved in growing up, we were able to begin to see how trauma and sexual abuse could create difficulties from early on.

Next, we moved on to explore the impact that childhood sexual abuse could have on adulthood. By thinking about development across the entire life span, we saw how childhood events could have an ongoing influence on adulthood. By the end of these sections of the book, you would hopefully have been able to consider how the material related to you as an individual.

By looking at some of the technical terms and diagnoses that professionals use, you might now feel more confident to approach the people that can help you. By having a *common language*, you will be better placed to describe what is troubling you. This will help professionals to understand your difficulties and to identify the right course of treatment for you.

Having read through Part IV, you will also have a good idea of how some of the more popular forms of psychological therapy work and what to expect. Hopefully, you have been able to use this information to think about what kind of therapy is right for you.

Through considering the options, you might also have a good idea of what the focus of therapy should be for you. This can help you to have realistic expectations about what you want to get from therapy.

We explored the ground rules for therapy. These are important because they will help you to find your way to therapy that is both safe and effective. You will also get to know more about what is expected of you in therapy and what you can do to help get the timing right. By being aware of the commitment that therapy requires, you are also helping yourself to prepare and to get the most from it (Bohart 2007).

By considering all of these issues, and reflecting upon how they relate to you as an individual, you will be helping yourself to make informed choices. This will help you on your way.

Further information, links and contacts

This section provides signposts to further information. This includes training organisations, accrediting bodies and various academic journals as well as voluntary organisations and a collection of links to other resources about mental health in general.

There is no limit to the amount of information available and each door that is opened will lead to new links. The suggestions below are offered as a manageable introductory list and as a starting point for those who wish to pursue further information. The details refer mainly to UK-based organisations. However, the websites given may provide signposts to services and organisations based outside the UK, where available.

Whilst many theories and methods have stood the test of time, new approaches are always being developed and new ideas are always coming to the fore. Therefore, what is offered here is correct at the time of going to press.

General health and mental health advice

Department of Health (DoH)

The Department of Health provides guidelines and protocols aimed at improving the quality of services provided by the NHS and social services in the UK. It is dedicated to setting national standards, profiling the way in which health and social care services should be delivered and promoting healthier living. The website provides access to a wealth of healthcare policy information and health-related population statistics.

Website: www.dh.gov.uk

Tel: 020 7210 4850

National Institute of Clinical Excellence (NICE)

NICE is an independent organisation providing national guidance on healthcare promotion and NHS service delivery in the UK. NICE provides treatment protocols for particular symptoms and conditions including Depression and PTSD as well as many more. The recommendations are evidence-based and are regularly updated and reviewed. The website contains a vast amount of information available through a search page as well as a dedicated A–Z to useful links.
Website: www.nice.org.uk
Email: nice@nice.org.uk
Tel: 0845 003 7780

National Library for Health (NLH)

The National Library for Health is an Internet-based library service available to all NHS staff. However, the service has also been extended to allow some public access. It provides a wide range of healthcare information accessed through a search page.
Website: www.library.nhs.uk

NHS Direct

NHS Direct is the official National Health Service information portal. It provides a 24-hour telephone helpline service in addition to a comprehensive website. The website has a self-help guide, a health encyclopaedia and a useful links section. It also has a search facility for more detailed local contact information.
Website: www.nhsdirect.nhs.uk
24-hour helpline: 0845 4647

Royal College of Psychiatrists (RCPsych)

The Royal College of Psychiatrists provides a website with a searchable database of useful mental health information.
Website: www.rcpsych.ac.uk
Email: rcpsych@rcpsych.ac.uk
Tel: 020 7235 2351

Drugs and alcohol

Alcohol Concern

Alcohol Concern is a national agency in the UK. Their remit is to reduce alcohol-related harm and promote the range and quality of services dedicated to helping those with alcohol-related problems. The website provides local contact information, a searchable knowledge base as well as an on-line bookshop and library.
Website: www.alcoholconcern.org.uk
Email: contact@alcoholconcern.org.uk
Tel: 020 7264 0510

DrugScope

DrugScope is a UK-based independent organisation and registered charity dedicated to providing information to the public as well as informing national policy development. The website is a good example of an information and signposting portal related to many aspects of drug misuse.
Website: www.drugscope.org.uk
Email: info@drugscope.org.uk
Tel: 020 7940 7500

Support organisations and networks

Mind

Mind is a registered charity providing information on all aspects of mental health to individuals, their families and to professionals. In England and Wales, Mind offers mental health services through a network of local Mind associations including sheltered homes, drop-in centres and counselling as well as advocacy and employment services. The website provides a very full A–Z directory of information along with a local service search facility.
Website: www.mind.org.uk
Email: contact@mind.org.uk
Tel: 020 8519 2122
Mindinfoline: 0845 766 0163

National Association for People Abused in Childhood (NAPAC)

NAPAC is a registered charity with a ten-year history of supporting those who have experienced abuse. The extensive website provides information about the freephone support line (see below) and also provides a contact service in the UK to help locate callers' nearest support group as well as many links to further information. NAPAC will also send out a resource pack containing legal advice and an extensive book list.

Website: www.napac.org.uk
Email: via website
Support line: 0800 085 3330

Survivors Trust

The Survivors Trust is a national organisation in the UK supporting voluntary sector services working with survivors of childhood sexual abuse and other forms of sexual violence. The website provides information on upcoming events and conferences and hosts a discussion forum.

Website: www.thesurvivorstrust.org
Email: via website

Therapist training and accrediting organisations

British Association for Behavioural and Cognitive Psychotherapies

Website: www.babcp.com
Email: babcp@babcp.com
Tel: 0161 797 4484

British Association for Counselling and Psychotherapy

Website: www.bacp.co.uk
Email: bacp@bacp.co.uk
Tel: 0870 443 5252

British Association of Psychotherapists

Website: www.bap-psychotherapy.org
Email: www.bap-psychotherapy.org/?&mailform
Tel: 020 8452 9823

British Psychoanalytic Council

Website: www.psychoanalytic-council.org
Email: mail@psychoanalytic-council.org
Tel: 020 7267 3626

British Psychological Society

Website: www.bps.org.uk
Email: enquiries@bps.org.uk
Tel: 0116 254 9568

Eye Movement Desensitisation and Reprocessing (EMDR)

Website: www.emdrassociation.org.uk
Email: emdrassociation@hotmail.com
Tel: 020 8343 3665

United Kingdom Council for Psychotherapy

Website: www.psychotherapy.org.uk
Email: info@psychotherapy.org.uk
Tel: 020 7014 9955

Selection of academic journals on research and the theory and practice of psychological therapy

Archives of General Psychiatry

Publisher: American Medical Association
Publisher website: archpsyc.ama-assn.org

Behaviour Research and Therapy

Publisher: Elsevier
Publisher website: www.elsevier.com

Behavioural and Cognitive Psychotherapy

Publisher: Cambridge University Press
Publisher website: journals.cambridge.org

British Journal of Clinical Psychology

Publisher: The British Psychological Society
Publisher website: www.bps.org.uk

British Journal of Developmental Psychology

Publisher: The British Psychological Society
Publisher website: www.bps.org.uk

Child Abuse & Neglect

Publisher: Elsevier
Publisher website: www.elsevier.com

Child Abuse Review

Publisher: Wiley
Publisher website: www3.interscience.wiley.com

Child Development

Publisher: Blackwell Publishing
Publisher website: www.blackwellpublishing.com

Clinical Psychology Review

Publisher: Elsevier
Publisher website: www.elsevier.com

Journal of Consulting and Clinical Psychology

Publisher: American Psychological Association
Publisher website: www.apa.org

Journal of Counseling Psychology

Publisher: American Psychological Association
Publisher website: www.apa.org

Journal of Psychotherapy Practice and Research

Publisher: American Psychiatric Association
Publisher website: www.psych.org

Journal of Traumatic Stress

Publisher: Wiley
Publisher website: www3.interscience.wiley.com

Psychological Bulletin

Publisher: American Psychological Association
Publisher website: www.apa.org

References

Part I Introduction and overview

Bagley, C. and Young, L. (1990) 'Depression, self-esteem and suicidal behavior as sequels of sexual abuse in childhood: research and therapy', in M. Rothery and G. Cameron (eds) *Child Maltreatment: Expanding Our Concept of Healing*, Hillsdale, NJ: Erlbaum.

Baker, A. W. and Duncan, S. P. (1985) 'Child sexual abuse: a study of prevalence in Great Britain', *Child Abuse and Neglect*, 9: 457–67.

Dobson, K. S. and Prout, P. (1998) 'Recovered memories of childhood sexual abuse: searching for the middle ground in clinical practice', *Canadian Psychology*, 39, 4: 257–65.

Fergusson, D. M. and Mullen, P. E. (1999) *Childhood Sexual Abuse: An Evidence Based Perspective*, London: Sage.

Finkelhor, D. (1994) 'The international epidemiology of child sexual abuse', *Child Abuse and Neglect*, 18, 5: 409–17.

Finkelhor, D. and Berliner, C. (1995) 'Research on the treatment of sexually abused children: a review and recommendations', *Journal of the American Academy of Child and Adolescent Psychiatry*, 34: 1408–23.

Finkelhor, D. and Browne, A. (1986) 'Initial and long-term effects: a conceptual framework', in D. Finkelhor (ed.) *A Sourcebook on Child Sexual Abuse*, Newbury Park, CA: Sage.

Finkelhor, D., Hotaling, G., Lewis, I. A. and Smith, C. (1990) 'Sexual abuse in a national survey of adult men and women: prevalence, characteristics and risk factors', *Child Abuse and Neglect*, 14: 19–28.

Gardner, R. A. (2004) 'The psychodynamics of patients with False Memory Syndrome (FMS)', *Journal of the American Academy of Psychoanalysis and Dynamic Psychiatry*, 32, 1: 77–90.

Hetzel, R. M. D., Brausch, A. M. and Montgomery, B. S. (2007) 'A meta-analytic investigation of therapy modality outcomes for sexually abused children and adolescents: an exploratory study', *Child Abuse and Neglect*, 31, 2: 125–41.

Hooper, P. D. (1990) 'Psychological sequelae of sexual abuse in childhood', *British Journal of General Practice*, 40: 29–31.

Kendler, K. S., Kuhn, J. W. and Prescott, C. A. (2004) 'Childhood sexual abuse, stressful life events and risk for major depression in women', *Psychological Medicine*, 34: 1475–82.

Merskey, H. (1996) 'Ethical issues in the search for repressed memories', *American Journal of Psychotherapy*, 50, 3: 323–35.

Mott, A. (2003) 'Child sexual abuse', in M. J. Bannon and Y. H. Carter (eds) *Protecting Children From Abuse and Neglect in Primary Care*, Oxford: Oxford University Press.

National Statistics (2007) *Population Estimates*. Online. Available at: <http://www.statistics.gov.uk> (accessed 23 May 2007).

Oaksford, K. L. and Frude, N. (2001) 'The prevalence and nature of child sexual abuse: evidence from a female university sample in the UK', *Child Abuse Review*, 10: 49–59.

Peters, S. D., Wyatt, G. E. and Finkelhor, D. (1986) 'Prevalence', in D. Finkelhor (ed.) *A Sourcebook on Child Sexual Abuse*, Newbury Park, CA: Sage.

Russell, D. E. (1986) *The Secret Trauma: Incest in the Lives of Girls and Women*, New York: Basic Books.

Summit, R. (1983) 'The child sexual abuse accommodation syndrome', *Child Abuse and Neglect*, 1: 177–93.

Ussher, J. M. and Dewberry, C. (1995) 'The nature and long-term effects of childhood sexual abuse: a survey of adult women survivors in Britain', *British Journal of Clinical Psychology*, 34: 177–92.

Wyatt, G. E. (1985) 'The sexual abuse of African American and European American women in childhood', *Child Abuse and Neglect*, 9: 507–19.

Wyatt, G. E., Loeb, T. B., Solis, B., Carmona, J. V. and Romero, G. (1999) 'The prevalence and circumstances of child sexual abuse: changes across a decade', *Child Abuse and Neglect*, 23, 1: 45–60.

Part II Child development

Ainsworth, M., Blehar, M., Waters, E. and Walls, S. (1978) *Patterns of Attachment: Assessed in the Strange Situation and at Home*, Hillsdale, NJ: Erlbaum.

Belsky, J. and Nezworski, T. (1988) *Clinical Implications of Attachment*, Hillsdale, NJ: Erlbaum.

Bowlby, J. (1988) *A Secure Base: Clinical Applications of Attachment Theory*, London: Routledge.

Carter, E. and McGoldrick, M. (1989) *The Changing Family Lifecycle: A Framework for Family Therapy*, 2nd edn, Boston: Allyn and Bacon.

Deblinger, E., Behl, L. E. and Glickman, A. R. (2006) 'Treating children who have experienced sexual abuse', in P. C. Kendall (ed.) *Child and Adolescent Therapy: Cognitive-Behavioral Procedures*, New York: Guilford Press.

Erikson, E. (1950) *Childhood and Society*, New York: Norton.

Erikson, E. (1959) *Identity and the Life Cycle*, New York: Norton.

Farmer, E. and Pollock, S. (2005) 'Managing sexually abused and/or abusing children in substitute care', *Child and Family Social Work*, 8, 2: 101–12.

Fergusson, D. M. and Mullen, P. E. (1999) *Childhood Sexual Abuse: An Evidence Based Perspective*, London: Sage.

Finkelhor, D. and Berliner, L. (1995) 'Research on the treatment of sexually abused children: a review and recommendations', *Journal of the American Academy of Child and Adolescent Psychiatry*, 34: 1408–23.

Finkelhor, D. and Browne, A. (1986a) 'Initial and long-term effects: a conceptual framework', in D. Finkelhor (ed.) *A Sourcebook on Child Sexual Abuse*, Newbury Park, CA: Sage.

Finkelhor, D. and Browne, A. (1986b) 'Initial and long-term effects: a review of the research', in D. Finkelhor (ed.) *A Sourcebook on Child Sexual Abuse*, Newbury Park, CA: Sage.

Grossman, K. and Grossman, K. (1991) 'Attachment quality as an organiser of emotional and behavioural responses in a longitudinal perspective', in C. M. Parkes, J. Stevenson-Hinde and P. Marris (eds) *Attachment Across the Life Cycle*, London: Routledge.

Horvath, A. O. and Greenberg, L. S. (1994) *The Working Alliance: Theory, Research and Practice*, New York: Wiley.

Horvath, A. O. and Symonds, B. D. (1991) 'Relation between working alliance and outcome in psychotherapy: a meta-analysis', *Journal of Counseling Psychology*, 38: 139–49.

Kendall-Tackett, K. A., Williams, L. M. and Finkelhor, D. (1993) 'Impact of sexual abuse on children: a review and synthesis of recent empirical studies', *Psychological Bulletin*, 113: 164–80.

Main, M. and Cassidy, J. (1988) 'Categories of response with the parent at age six: predicted from infant attachment classifications and stable over a one month period', *Developmental Psychology*, 24: 415–26.

Noelting, G. (1980a) 'The development of proportional reasoning and the ratio concept. Part I: The differentiation of stages', *Educational Studies in Mathematics*, 11: 217–54.

Noelting, G. (1980b) 'The development of proportional reasoning and the ratio concept. Part II: Problem structure at successive stages: problem-solving strategies and the mechanism of adaptive restructuring', *Educational Studies in Mathematics*, 11: 331–63.

Piaget, J. (1952) *The Origin of Intelligence in the Child*, London: Routledge and Kegan Paul.

Sperry, D. M. and Gilbert, B. O. (2005) 'Child peer sexual abuse: preliminary data on outcomes and disclosure experiences', *Child Abuse and Neglect*, 8: 889–904.

van Ijzendoorn, M. H. (1995) 'Adult attachment representations, parental responsiveness, and infant attachment: a meta-analysis on the predictive validity of the Adult Attachment Interview', *Psychological Bulletin*, 117, 3: 387–403.

van Ijzendoorn, M. H. and Kroonenburg, P. M. (1988) 'Cross cultural patterns of attachment: a meta-analysis of the strange situation', *Child Development*, 59: 147–56.

Vaughn, B. E., Egeland, B., Sroufe, L. A. and Waters, E. (1979) 'Individual differences in infant–mother attachment at twelve and eighteen months: stability and change in families under stress', *Child Development*, 50: 971–5.

Waters, E., Hamilton, C. E. and Weinfield, N. S. (2000) 'The stability of attachment security from infancy to adolescence and early adulthood: general introduction', *Child Development*, 71: 678–83.

Young, J. E., Klosko, J. S. and Weishaar, M. (2003) *Schema Therapy: A Practitioner's Guide*, New York: Guilford Press.

Part III Adult development

APA (1980) *Diagnostic and Statistical Manual of Mental Disorders*, Third Edition, Text Revision, Washington, DC: American Psychiatric Association.

APA (2000) *Diagnostic and Statistical Manual of Mental Disorders*, Fourth Edition, Text Revision, Washington, DC: American Psychiatric Association.

Bell, L. (2003) *Managing Intense Emotions and Overcoming Self-Destructive Habits: A Self-Help Manual*, Hove: Brunner-Routledge.

Bolton, D., Dearsley, P., Madronal-Lugue, R. and Baron-Cohen, S. (2002) 'Magical thinking in childhood and adolescence: development and relation to obsessive-compulsion', *British Journal of Developmental Psychology*, 20: 479–94.

van Egmund, J. J. (2003) 'Multiple meanings of secondary gain', *The American Journal of Psychoanalysis*, 63, 2: 137–47.

Ehlers, A. and Clark, D. M. (2000) 'A cognitive model of Post-Traumatic Stress Disorder', *Behaviour Research and Therapy*, 38: 319–45.

Einstein, D. A. (2006) 'Magical thinking in Obsessive-Compulsive Disorder, Panic Disorder and the general community', *Behavioural and Cognitive Psychotherapy*, 34, 3: 351–7.

Erikson, E. (1950) *Childhood and Society*, New York: Norton.

Erikson, E. (1959) *Identity and the Life Cycle*, New York: Norton.

Fergusson, D. M. and Mullen, P. E. (1999) *Childhood Sexual Abuse: An Evidence Based Perspective*, London: Sage.

Foa, E. B. and Meadows, E. A. (1997) 'Psychosocial treatments for Post-Traumatic Stress Disorder: a critical review', *Annual Review of Psychology*, 48: 449–80.

Fossati, A., Madeddu, F. and Maffei, C. (1999) 'Borderline Personality Disorder and childhood sexual abuse: a meta-analytic study', *Journal of Personality Disorders*, 13, 3: 268–80.

Giaconia, R. M., Reinherz, H. Z., Silverman, A. B., Pakiz, B., Frost, A. K. and Cohen, E. (1995) 'Traumas and Post-Traumatic Stress Disorder in a community population of older adolescents', *Journal of the American Academy of Child and Adolescent Psychiatry*, 34, 10: 1369–80.

Hegadoren, K. M., Lasiuk, G. C. and Coupland, N. J. (2006) 'Post-Traumatic Stress Disorder part III: health effects of interpersonal violence among women', *Perspectives in Psychiatric Care*, 42, 3: 163–73.

Herman, J. L. (1992) *Trauma and Recovery*, New York: Basic Books.

Johnson, D. M., Sheahan, T. C. and Chard, K. M. (2003) 'Personality disorders, coping and Post-Traumatic Stress Disorder in women with histories of childhood sexual abuse', *Journal of Child Sexual Abuse*, 12, 2: 19–39.

Johnson, J. G., Smailes, E. M., Cohen, P., Brown, M. D. and Bernstein, D. (2000) 'Associations between four types of childhood neglect and Personality Disorder symptoms during adolescence and early adulthood: findings of a community based longitudinal study', *Journal of Personality Disorders*, 14, 2: 171–87.

Kessler, R. C., Sonnega, A., Bromet, E., Hughes, M. and Nelson, C. B. (1995) 'Post-Traumatic Stress Disorder in the National Comorbidity Survey', *Archives of General Psychiatry*, 52, 12: 1048–60.

Lochner, C., Du Toit, P. L., Zungu, D. N., Marais, A., Van Kradenburg, J., Seedat, S., Niehaus, D. J. and Stein, D. J. (2002) 'Childhood trauma in Obsessive-Compulsive Disorder, Trichotillomania and controls', *Depression and Anxiety*, 15, 2: 66–8.

McLean, L. M. (2003) 'Implications of childhood sexual abuse for adult Borderline Personality Disorder and Complex Post-Traumatic Stress Disorder', *American Journal of Psychiatry*, 160, 2: 369–71.

Moulding, R. (2006) 'Anxiety disorders and control related beliefs: the exemplar of Obsessive-Compulsive Disorder (OCD)', *Clinical Psychology Review*, 26, 5: 573–83.

Narrow, W. E., Rae, D. S., Robins, L. N. and Regier, D. A. (2002) 'Revised prevalence estimates of mental disorders in the United States: using a clinical significance criterion to reconcile two surveys' estimates', *Archives of General Psychiatry*, 59: 115–23.

Ogata, S. N., Silk, K. R., Goodrich, S., Lohr, N., Westen, D. and Hill, E. M. (1990) 'Childhood sexual and physical abuse in adult patients with Borderline Personality Disorder', *American Journal of Psychiatry*, 147, 8: 1008–13.

Ouimette, P. and Brown, P. J. (eds) (2003) *Trauma and Substance Abuse: Causes, Consequences and Treatment of Co-morbid Disorders*, Washington, DC: American Psychiatric Association.

PDM Task Force (2006) *Psychodynamic Diagnostic Manual*, Silver Spring, MD: Alliance of Psychoanalytic Organizations.

Resnick, H. S., Kilpatrick, D. G., Dansky, B. S., Saunders, B. E. and Best, C. L. (1993) 'Prevalence of civilian trauma and Post-traumatic Stress Disorder in a representative national sample of women', *Journal of Consulting and Clinical Psychology*, 61: 984–91.

Roth, S., Newman, E., Pelcovitz, D., van der Kolk, B. A. and Mandel, F. S. (1997) 'Complex PTSD in victims exposed to sexual and physical abuse:

results from the DSM-IV Field Trial for Posttraumatic Stress Disorder', *Journal of Traumatic Stress*, 539–55.

Siegel, D. J. (1995) 'Memory, trauma and psychotherapy: a cognitive science view', *Journal of Psychotherapy Practice and Research*, 4: 93–122.

Silk, K. R., Lee, S., Hill, E. M. and Lohr, N. E. (1995) 'Borderline Personality Disorder symptoms and severity of sexual abuse', *American Journal of Psychiatry*, 152, 7: 1059–64.

Sinason, V. (2002) *Attachment, Trauma and Multiplicity: Working with Dissociative Disorder*, London: Routledge.

Sugarman, S. (1987) *Piaget's Construction of the Child's Reality*, Cambridge: Cambridge University Press.

World Health Organization (1993) *International Statistical Classification of Disease and Related Health Problems*, 10th Revision, Geneva: WHO.

Part IV Psychological therapy

Bateman, A. and Holmes, J. (1995) *Introduction to Psychoanalysis: Contemporary Theory and Practice*, London: Routledge.

Beck, A. T. (1970) 'Cognitive Therapy, nature and relation to Behaviour Therapy', *Behaviour Therapy*, 1: 184–200.

Beck, A. T. (1976) *Cognitive Therapy and the Emotional Disorders*, New York: International Universities Press.

Beck, A. T., Steer, R. A. and Garbin, M. C. (1988a) 'Psychometric properties of the Beck Depression Inventory: twenty-five years of evaluation', *Clinical Psychology Review*, 8: 77–100.

Beck, A. T., Epstein, N., Brown, G. and Steer R. A. (1988b) 'An inventory for measuring clinical anxiety: psychometric properties', *Journal of Consulting and Clinical Psychology*, 56: 893–7.

Bohart, A. C. (2007) 'Insight and the active client', in L. G. Castonquay and C. Hill (eds) *Insight in Psychotherapy*, Washington, DC: American Psychological Association.

Brown, D. and Pedder, J. (1991) *Introduction to Psychotherapy: An Outline of Psychodynamic Principles and Practice*, London: Routledge.

Carlson, E. B. and Putnam, F. W. (1992) *Manual for the Dissociative Experiences Scale*, Beloit, WI: Eve Bernstein, Department of Psychology, Beloit College. See also Turner, S. and Lee, D. (1998). *Measures in Post Traumatic Stress Disorder: a practitioner's guide*. London: Nelson Publishing Company Ltd.

Chemtob, C. M., Tolin, D. F., van der Kolk, B. A. and Pitman, R. K. (2000) 'Eye movement desensitization and reprocessing', in E. B. Foa, T. M. Keane and M. J. Friedman (eds) *Effective Treatments for PTSD: Practice Guidelines from the International Society for Traumatic Stress Studies*, New York: Guilford Press.

Department of Health (2001) *Treatment Choice in Psychological Therapies and*

182   *References*

Counselling: Evidence Based Clinical Practice Guideline, London: Department of Health.
Derogatis, L. R. and Spencer, P. M. (1982) *Brief Symptom Inventory: Administration, Scoring and Procedures Manual*, Baltimore: Clinical Psychometric Research.
De Shazer, S. (1985) *Keys to Solution in Brief Therapy*, New York: Norton.
Ellis, A. (1962) *Reason and Emotion in Psychotherapy*, New York: Lyle Stuart.
Freud, S. (1894) 'The neuro-psychoses of defence (I)', *Standard Edition of the Complete Psychological Works of Sigmund Freud*, Vol. 3, London: Hogarth Press and the Institute of Psychoanalysis.
Freud, S. and Breuer, J. (1895) 'Studies on hysteria', *Standard Edition of the Complete Psychological Works of Sigmund Freud*, Vol. 2, London: Hogarth Press and the Institute of Psychoanalysis.
Goldberg, D. P. (1978) *Manual of the General Health Questionnaire*, Windsor: NFER.
Padesky, C. A. and Greenberger, D. (1995) *Clinician's Guide to Mind over Mood*, New York: Guilford Press.
Greenson, R. R. (1965) 'The working alliance and the transference neurosis', *Psychoanalytic Quarterly*, 34: 155–81.
Hawton, K., Salkovskis, P. M., Kirk, J. and Clark, D. (1996) *Cognitive Behaviour Therapy for Psychiatric Problems: A Practical Guide*, Oxford: Oxford University Press.
Horowitz, M. H. (1987) 'Some notes on insight and its failures', *Psycho-analytic Quarterly*, 56: 177–98.
Horowitz, M. J., Wilner, N. and Alvarez, W. (1979) 'Impact of Event Scale: a measure of subjective distress', *Psychosomatic Medicine*, 41: 207–18.
Horvath, A. O. and Symonds, B. D. (1991) 'Relation between working alliance and outcome in psychotherapy', *Journal of Counseling Psychology*, 38: 139–49.
Mahler, M., Pine, F. and Bergman, A. (1975) *The Psychological Birth of the Human Infant*, London: Hutchinson.
Malan, D. (1979) *Individual Psychotherapy and the Science of Psychodynamics*, London: Butterworth.
Meichenbaum, D. H. (1975) 'Self-instructional methods', in F. H. Kanfer and A. P. Goldstein (eds) *Helping People Change: A Textbook of Methods*, New York: Pergamon.
Mellor-Clark, J. and Barkham, M. (1998) 'Effectiveness, evaluation and audit of counselling in primary care', in L. Rain (ed.) *A Practical Guide to Counselling in Primary Care*, London: Sage.
Michalak, J. and Holtforth, M. G. (2006) 'Where do we go from here? The goal perspective in psychotherapy', *Clinical Psychology: Science and Practice*, 13, 4: 346–65.
National Institute of Clinical Excellence (2005) *The Management of PTSD in Adults and Children in Primary and Secondary Care*, London: NICE.
Rogers, C. (1951) *Client-Centred Therapy*, Boston: Houghton Mifflin.

Roth, A. and Fonagy, P. (1996) *What Works for Whom? A Critical Review of Psychotherapy Research*, New York: Guilford Press.

Salkovskis, P. M. (ed.) (1996) *Frontiers of Cognitive Therapy*, New York: Guilford Press.

Sandler, J., Dare, C. and Holder, A. (1992) *The Patient and the Analyst*, London: Karnac.

Shapiro, F. (1995) *Eye Movement Desensitization and Reprocessing: Basic Principles, Protocols and Procedures*, New York: Guilford Press.

Skinner, B. F. (1953) *Science and Human Behavior*, New York: Macmillan.

Snaith, R. P. and Zigmond, A. S. (1983) 'The Hospital Anxiety and Depression Scale', *Acta Psychiatrica Scandinavica*, 67: 361–70.

Tarrier, N., Wells, A. and Haddock, G. (1998) *Treating Complex Cases: The Cognitive-Behavioural Therapy Approach*, Chichester: Wiley.

Young, J. E., Klosko, J. S. and Weishaar, M. E. (2003) *Schema Therapy: A Practitioner's Guide*, New York: Guilford Press.

Index

sudden changes in behaviour 61, 62, 66
suffocation 65
suicidal ideation 100
suicide and suicidal thoughts and feelings: adulthood 25, 99–100; childhood 62, 87; depression 89; high incidence 13; Personality Disorder 102, 114; PTSD 104, 118
support groups and networks 154–5, 165, 171–2
supportive therapy 132
Survivors Trust 172
symptoms 21, 27, 28, 87–102, 119–20, 131
systematic desensitisation 119

teenagers: *see* adolescence
temperament 44, 54
theory of mind 51
therapists: boundaries 149, 151; professional registration and accreditation 150, 172–3; relationship with client 55, 132–3, 149; training 147; what to expect from 150–1
therapy: *see* psychological therapy
thought–feeling–behaviour chains 110–11
thoughts 8, 16, 27, 28, 49–54, 64, 105, 106–8, 137–8
threat 13, 15, 16, 22, 75, 94, 105
tics 61
total refusal syndrome 63
training and training organisations 29, 147, 172–3

trauma 54
trauma-focused psychological therapy 105, 109, 110
traumagenic dynamics 23–4, 72–3
treats 71, 73
triggers 138
truancy 63
trust 24, 45–6, 54, 56–7, 84, 107, 139, 142, 156, 159
'tuned in' parents 46, 47, 56, 57
twitching 90

under-reporting of abuse 17
United Kingdom Council for Psychotherapy (UKCP) 150, 173
unsafe sex 114
urination, pain on 65

valuing oneself 12–13
victimisation 54
vigilance 108
violence 13, 16, 44
visible signs of abuse 65
visual imagery 144
voluntary sector 154
vulnerability 56; to stress 114, 115

weight 88, 95–6
withdrawal 21, 23, 24, 27, 56, 57, 61, 62, 63, 66, 71, 89, 95, 98, 118
working alliance and psychological therapy 55, 132–3
worry 90
worthless 74, 88, 95, 100
wounding 65
writing things down 8, 73, 157